D0295008

flavours of italy

70 easy authentic recipes

PLEASE NOTE that the cup and spoon measurements used in this book are metric. A conversion chart appears on page 126.

This edition first published in 2008 by
ACP Magazines Ltd
Exclusively for Marks and Spencer plc

www.marksandspencer.com

First published 2008

ISBN: 978-1-903777-19-0

Printed and bound in China

contents

rocket and pancetta soup

PREPARATION TIME 20 MINUTES COOKING TIME 35 MINUTES

100g thinly sliced pancetta
1 tablespoon olive oil
1 medium red onion (170g), chopped coarsely
2 cloves garlic, quartered
1½ tablespoons balsamic vinegar
4 medium potatoes (800g), chopped coarsely
3 cups (750ml) chicken stock
3 cups (750ml) water
500g rocket, trimmed
¼ cup (20g) finely grated parmesan cheese

1 Place pancetta in single layer on oven tray. Bake, uncovered, in moderate oven, about 15 minutes or until crisp. Drain pancetta on absorbent paper; chop coarsely.
2 Heat oil in large saucepan; cook onion and garlic, stirring, until onion softens. Add vinegar and potato; cook, stirring, 5 minutes.
3 Add stock and the water; bring to a boil. Reduce heat; simmer, uncovered, about 15 minutes or until potato softens. Stir in rocket; cook, stirring, about 2 minutes or until rocket wilts.
4 Blend or process soup mixture, in batches, until smooth. Return soup to cleaned saucepan; stir over heat until hot. Divide soup among serving bowls; sprinkle with cheese and pancetta.

SERVES 6
PER SERVING 7G FAT; 855KJ (204 CAL)

tuscan bean soup

PREPARATION TIME 25 MINUTES (PLUS SOAKING AND STANDING TIME)
COOKING TIME 1 HOUR 40 MINUTES

1½ cups (300g) dried haricot beans
1 tablespoon olive oil
1 medium brown onion (150g), chopped coarsely
2 cloves garlic, crushed
2 trimmed sticks celery (150g), chopped coarsely
1 medium carrot (120g), chopped coarsely
2 bacon rashers (140g), chopped coarsely
4 large ripe tomatoes (1kg), peeled, chopped coarsely
1.5 litres (6 cups) vegetable stock
1 teaspoon sugar
¼ cup fresh parsley sprigs
¼ cup (70g) tomato paste

1 Cover beans with water in large bowl; stand, covered, overnight.
2 Heat oil in large saucepan; cook onion, garlic, celery, carrot and bacon, stirring, until vegetables are just tender.
3 Add tomato; cook, stirring, about 5 minutes or until tomato is soft.
4 Stir in rinsed drained beans, stock, sugar, parsley and paste; bring to a boil. Reduce heat; simmer, covered, about 1½ hours or until beans are tender.
[Can be made a day ahead and refrigerated, covered or frozen for up to 2 months.]

SERVES 4
PER SERVING 16.8G FAT; 3060KJ (731 CAL)

minestrone

PREPARATION TIME 25 MINUTES (PLUS SOAKING TIME)
COOKING TIME 1 HOUR 10 MINUTES

1/2 cup (100g) dried cannellini beans
2 teaspoons olive oil
1 medium brown onion (150g), chopped finely
2 cloves garlic, crushed
10 slices prosciutto (150g), chopped coarsely
1 trimmed stick celery (75g), chopped finely
1 medium carrot (120g), chopped finely
1 medium green courgette (120g), chopped finely
800g canned tomatoes
1.5 litres (6 cups) chicken stock
1 medium potato (200g), chopped finely
1 cup (170g) ditalini
1 cup (80g) loosely packed finely shredded savoy cabbage
1 cup loosely packed, finely shredded spinach leaves
1 tablespoon finely shredded fresh basil
1/2 cup (40g) grated parmesan cheese

1 Place beans in medium bowl; cover with water. Stand overnight; drain.
2 Heat oil in large saucepan; cook onion and garlic, stirring, until onion is soft. Add prosciutto, celery, carrot and courgette; cook, stirring, 5 minutes. Stir in undrained crushed tomatoes and stock; bring to a boil. Reduce heat; simmer, uncovered, 30 minutes.
3 Stir in beans and potato; simmer, uncovered, 15 minutes. [Can be made a day ahead to this stage and refrigerated, covered, or frozen for up to 3 months.]
4 Add pasta; simmer, uncovered, about 10 minutes or until pasta is tender.
5 Just before serving, stir in cabbage, spinach and basil; serve soup sprinkled with cheese.

SERVES 6
PER SERVING 8.7G FAT; 1472KJ (352 CAL)

TIPS Macaroni or any small tubular pasta can be substituted for the ditalini. Make basic soup mixture (up to and including step 3) when you soak the beans (ie, the day before required), to allow the flavours to develop. Top each bowl of soup with a teaspoon of basil pesto, to make minestrone genovese.

lentil soup

PREPARATION TIME 15 MINUTES COOKING TIME 1 HOUR 25 MINUTES

1/4 cup (60ml) olive oil
1 large brown onion (200g), chopped coarsely
1 medium aubergine (300g), quartered
4 medium tomatoes (760g), quartered
1 large red pepper (350g), quartered
3 cloves garlic, peeled
2 litres (8 cups) vegetable stock
1 cup (200g) puy lentils
1/2 cup (125ml) sour cream
2 tablespoons finely chopped fresh chives

1 Combine oil, onion, aubergine, tomato, pepper and garlic in large baking dish. Bake, uncovered, in hot oven about 45 minutes or until vegetables are tender. Turn once halfway through cooking.
2 Place pepper pieces on plate, skin-side up. Cover; stand 5 minutes. Peel pepper, tomato and aubergine; discard skin. Chop flesh coarsely keeping each vegetable separate.
3 Blend or process aubergine with garlic and onion until pureed; combine with stock and lentils in large saucepan. Bring to a boil; reduce heat; simmer, uncovered, about 35 minutes or until lentils are tender. [Can be made a day ahead to this stage and refrigerated, covered.]
4 Add pepper and tomato; stir over heat until hot. Divide soup among serving bowls. Dollop each with sour cream; sprinkle with chives.

SERVES 6
PER SERVING 19.2G FAT; 1409KJ (337 CAL)

TIP Brown lentils can be substituted for the puy lentils, although they do require longer cooking.

marinated olives with rosemary and thyme

PREPARATION TIME 10 MINUTES (PLUS MARINATING TIME)
COOKING TIME 5 MINUTES

200g green olives, drained
200g black olives, drained
2 tablespoons fresh thyme
$^1/_3$ cup fresh rosemary
2 cloves garlic, sliced thinly
$2^1/_2$ cups (625ml) olive oil
$^1/_2$ cup (125ml) lemon juice

1 Layer olives, herbs and garlic into hot sterilised 1-litre (4 cup) jar.
2 Gently heat oil and juice in medium saucepan; do not boil. Pour enough of the oil mixture into jar to cover olives, leaving 1cm space between olives and top of jar; seal while hot.

MAKES 4 CUPS
PER SERVING 17.3G FAT; 727KJ (174 CAL)
STORE RECIPE BEST MADE 3 DAYS AHEAD; CAN BE REFRIGERATED FOR UP TO 3 MONTHS.

TIP Oil will solidify on refrigeration; bring to room temperature before serving.

marinated aubergine

PREPARATION TIME 15 MINUTES (PLUS STANDING AND MARINATING TIME)
COOKING TIME 10 MINUTES

10 baby aubergines (600g)
coarse cooking salt
1 litre (4 cups) white vinegar
2 cups (500ml) water
1 tablespoon coarsely chopped fresh mint
1 teaspoon dried thyme
1 clove garlic, sliced thinly
1 fresh red thai chilli, deseeded, chopped finely
½ teaspoon ground black pepper
1½ cups (375ml) hot olive oil

1 Quarter aubergines lengthways; place in colander. Sprinkle with salt; stand 1 hour. Rinse aubergines under cold running water; drain on absorbent paper.
2 Heat vinegar, the water and 2 teaspoons of the salt in large saucepan until hot; do not boil.
3 Add aubergines; simmer, uncovered, 5 minutes. Drain; discard vinegar mixture.
4 Combine herbs, garlic, chilli, pepper and oil in large heatproof bowl.
5 Place aubergines upright in hot sterilised 1-litre (4 cup) jar. Carefully top with enough oil mixture to cover aubergines, leaving 1cm space between aubergines and top of jar; seal while hot.

MAKES 40 PIECES
PER SERVING 2.8G FAT; 128KJ (31 CAL)
STORE RECIPE BEST MADE 3 DAYS AHEAD; CAN BE REFRIGERATED FOR UP TO 3 MONTHS.

carpaccio with fresh herbs

PREPARATION TIME 25 MINUTES (PLUS FREEZING TIME)

500g piece of beef eye-fillet, about 6cm diameter
$\frac{1}{3}$ cup (80ml) extra virgin olive oil
$\frac{1}{4}$ cup (60ml) lemon juice
$\frac{1}{4}$ cup firmly packed fresh basil
$\frac{1}{4}$ cup firmly packed fresh flat-leaf parsley
1 tablespoon fresh oregano
1 tablespoon coarsely chopped fresh chives
$\frac{1}{4}$ cup (25g) drained sun-dried tomatoes, sliced thinly
2 tablespoons flaked parmesan cheese
freshly ground black pepper

1 Remove any excess fat from beef. Wrap beef tightly in plastic wrap; freeze about $1\frac{1}{2}$ hours or until partly frozen.
2 Cut beef into 1mm slices; freeze until required. [Store in freezer container, between layers of freezer wrap, for up to 2 months.]
3 Just before serving, place beef on serving plate. Drizzle with oil and juice; top with combined herbs, tomato, cheese and pepper.

TIPS Sashimi-quality tuna can be used in place of the beef; ask the fishmonger to slice tuna, paper-thin, for you. Omit the parmesan and add a sprinkling of baby capers.

SERVES 8
PER SERVING 12.9G FAT; 747KJ (178 CAL)

roasted tomatoes with garlic and herbs

PREPARATION TIME 10 MINUTES COOKING TIME 1 HOUR

- 9 large plum tomatoes (1.2kg), halved
- 1 tablespoon extra virgin olive oil
- 1 teaspoon sea salt
- 1 teaspoon cracked black pepper
- 8 sprigs fresh thyme
- 2 cloves garlic, peeled, sliced thinly
- 2 teaspoons finely chopped fresh oregano
- 1 teaspoon finely chopped fresh thyme, extra
- 2 tablespoons extra virgin olive oil, extra

1 Place tomatoes in large baking dish with oil, salt, pepper, thyme and garlic.

2 Bake in moderately hot oven about 1 hour or until tender and browned lightly.

3 Drizzle with combined oregano, extra thyme and extra oil. Serve warm or cold.

SERVES 6

PER SERVING 9.3G FAT; 448KJ (107 CAL)

STORE RECIPE CAN BE MADE 3 DAYS AHEAD AND REFRIGERATED, COVERED.

beans with tomato

PREPARATION TIME 35 MINUTES COOKING TIME 40 MINUTES

- 30g butter
- 1 clove garlic, crushed
- 45g can anchovy fillets, drained, chopped finely
- 2 medium brown onions (300g), chopped finely
- 3 medium tomatoes (570g), chopped finely
- 1 tablespoon tomato paste
- 2 teaspoons finely chopped fresh basil
- 1/2 teaspoon sugar
- 1kg borlotti beans, shelled
- 1 cup (250ml) water
- 2 teaspoons finely shredded fresh basil, extra

1 Melt butter in large saucepan; cook garlic, anchovy, onion and tomato until onion is transparent. Add paste, basil, sugar and beans; mix until well combined.

2 Add the water; bring to a boil. Reduce heat; simmer, covered, about 30 minutes or until beans are tender. Stir through extra basil.

TIPS 600g canned borlotti or cannellini beans can be substituted for the shelled borlotti beans; rinse and drain beans before adding for last 10 minutes of cooking. Recipe can be made 2 days ahead and refrigerated, covered; reheat or bring to room temperature before serving.

SERVES 6

PER SERVING 8.2G FAT; 2080KJ (497 CAL)

baked mushrooms

PREPARATION TIME 15 MINUTES COOKING TIME 10 MINUTES

9 medium flat mushrooms (900g)
60g butter, melted
3 bacon rashers (210g), chopped finely
4 spring onions, chopped finely
2 cloves garlic, crushed
2 tablespoons stale breadcrumbs
1 tablespoon cream
2 teaspoons fresh oregano, chopped coarsely
2 tablespoons grated parmesan cheese

1 Gently remove stalks from eight of the mushrooms. Finely chop stalks and remaining mushroom.
2 Brush mushroom caps all over with butter. Place on lightly greased oven trays.
3 Cook bacon and onion in small non-stick frying pan until bacon is crisp. Add chopped mushroom, garlic and breadcrumbs. Cook, stirring, until well combined. Remove from heat; stir in cream, oregano and cheese. Divide bacon mixture between mushroom caps. [Can be made 3 hours ahead to this stage and refrigerated, covered.]
4 Bake in moderately hot oven about 10 minutes or until hot.

SERVES 4
PER SERVING 17.4G FAT; 990KJ (236 CAL)

TIP Cap mushrooms can be substituted for the flat mushrooms. Cook 5 minutes; cool slightly before serving.

roasted pepper and prosciutto bruschetta

PREPARATION TIME 20 MINUTES COOKING TIME 7 MINUTES

- 1/2 loaf ciabatta (275g)
- 3 cloves garlic, halved
- 1/4 cup (60ml) olive oil
- 2 medium red peppers (400g)
- 5 prosciutto slices (75g), chopped coarsely
- 1 tablespoon balsamic vinegar
- 2 tablespoons fresh oregano

1 Cut ciabatta into 1.5cm thick slices; halve any large slices crossways. Toast under hot grill until browned lightly; while still hot, rub one side of toast with garlic. Place toast in single layer on tray; drizzle oil evenly over toast. [Can be made 3 hours ahead to this stage and covered.]

2 Quarter peppers; remove and discard seeds and membranes. Place pepper on oven tray; roast under hot grill or in very hot oven, skin-side up, until skin blisters and blackens. Cover pepper pieces in plastic 5 minutes. Peel away skin; discard. Cut pepper into thin strips.

3 Cook prosciutto in medium heated non-stick frying pan until crisp. Add pepper and vinegar to pan; stir to combine. Cool to room temperature.

4 Just before serving divide pepper mixture among bruschetta; top with oregano.

SERVES 8

PER SERVING 8.4G FAT; 695KJ (166 CAL)

bruschetta with creamy mushrooms

PREPARATION TIME 20 MINUTES COOKING TIME 15 MINUTES

½ loaf ciabatta (275g)
4 cloves garlic, halved
½ cup (125ml) olive oil
250g flat mushrooms, chopped finely
1 tablespoon lemon juice
½ cup (125ml) cream
125g button mushrooms, sliced thinly
2 tablespoons finely grated parmesan cheese
¼ cup coarsely chopped fresh chives

1 Cut ciabatta into 1.5cm thick slices; halve any large slices crossways. Toast under hot grill until browned lightly; while still hot, rub one side of toast with three cloves of the garlic. Place toast in single layer on tray; drizzle half of the oil evenly over toast. [Can be made 3 hours ahead to this stage and covered.]
2 Crush remaining garlic. Heat remaining oil in medium non-stick frying pan; cook flat mushrooms, stirring over heat, until very soft. Add juice; stir over high heat until absorbed. Pour in cream; stir to combine. Gently stir in button mushrooms; stir over high heat until almost all liquid is absorbed. Remove from heat; stir in cheese.
3 Just before serving, top bruschetta with mushroom mixture; sprinkle with chives.

SERVES 8
PER SERVING 22.7G FAT; 1221KJ (292 CAL)

olive, anchovy and caper bruschetta

PREPARATION TIME 15 MINUTES COOKING TIME 5 MINUTES

1/2 loaf ciabatta (275g)
3 cloves garlic, halved
1/3 cup (80ml) olive oil
3 anchovy fillets, drained, chopped finely
1/2 cup (60g) seeded black olives, chopped finely
1 tablespoon drained baby capers
1 tablespoon lemon juice
1/3 cup (25g) parmesan cheese flakes
2 tablespoons marjoram

1 Cut ciabatta into 1.5cm thick slices; halve any large slices crossways. Toast under hot grill until browned lightly; while still hot, rub one side of toast with garlic. Place toast in single layer on tray; drizzle 1/4 cup (60ml) of the oil evenly over toast. [Can be made 3 hours ahead to this stage and covered.]

2 Combine anchovy, olives, capers, juice and remaining oil in small bowl.

3 Just before serving, divide olive mixture among bruschetta; top with cheese then marjoram.

SERVES 8

PER SERVING 11.3G FAT; 792KJ (189 CAL)

bruschetta with tomato and rocket

PREPARATION TIME 15 MINUTES COOKING TIME 5 MINUTES

- 1/2 loaf ciabatta (275g)
- 3 cloves garlic, halved
- 1/4 cup (60ml) olive oil
- 3 medium plum tomatoes (225g), chopped finely
- 1/2 small red onion (50g), chopped finely
- 25g baby rocket leaves

1 Cut ciabatta into 1.5cm thick slices; halve any large slices crossways. Toast under hot grill until browned lightly; while still hot, rub one side of toast with garlic. Place toast in single layer on tray; drizzle oil evenly over toast. [Can be made 3 hours ahead to this stage and covered.]

2 Combine tomato and onion in small bowl.

3 Just before serving, top bruschetta with tomato mixture, then rocket; sprinkle with freshly ground black pepper, if desired.

SERVES 8

PER SERVING 7.8G FAT; 628KJ (150 CAL)

spaghetti bolognese

PREPARATION TIME **15 MINUTES** COOKING TIME **2 HOURS 15 MINUTES**

- 2 tablespoons olive oil
- 1 large brown onion (200g), chopped finely
- 750g minced beef
- 425g canned tomatoes
- 1 teaspoon fresh basil
- 1 teaspoon fresh oregano
- ½ teaspoon fresh thyme
- ⅓ cup (95g) tomato paste
- 1 litre (4 cups) water
- 250g spaghetti
- grated parmesan cheese

1 Heat oil in large saucepan; cook onion until golden brown. Add beef to pan; cook until beef browns, mashing with fork occasionally to break up lumps. Pour off any surplus fat.

2 Push undrained tomatoes through sieve; add to pan. Add herbs, paste and the water; bring to a boil. Reduce heat; simmer, very gently, uncovered, about 1½ hours, or until nearly all liquid evaporates. [Can be made 2 days ahead to this stage and refrigerated, covered, or frozen for up to 3 months.]

3 Cook spaghetti in large saucepan of boiling water until just tender; drain well.

4 Arrange hot spaghetti in individual serving bowls; top with sauce. Sprinkle with cheese.

SERVES **4**

PER SERVING **28.7G FAT; 1867KJ (446 CAL)**

TIP A true bolognese sauce contains no garlic, however two crushed cloves of garlic can be added to the tomatoes in step 2, if desired.

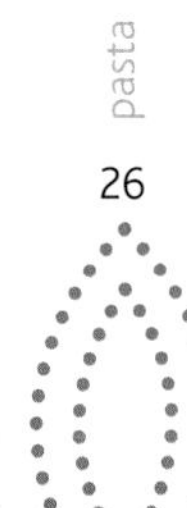

spaghetti napoletana

PREPARATION TIME 5 MINUTES COOKING TIME 25 MINUTES

2 teaspoons olive oil
1 small brown onion (80g), chopped finely
3 cloves garlic, crushed
850g canned tomatoes
1/4 cup coarsely chopped, firmly packed fresh basil
1/3 cup coarsely chopped, firmly packed fresh flat-leaf parsley
375g spaghetti

1 Heat oil in large saucepan; cook onion and garlic, stirring, until onion softens.
2 Add undrained crushed tomatoes; bring to a boil. Reduce heat; simmer, uncovered, about 20 minutes or until reduced by about a third. Stir in basil and parsley. [Can be made a day ahead to this stage and refrigerated, covered, or frozen for up to 3 months.]
3 Meanwhile, cook pasta in large saucepan of boiling water, uncovered, until just tender; drain. Serve pasta topped with sauce.

SERVES 4
PER SERVING 4G FAT; 1666KJ (398 CAL)

TIP If you cook this sauce even longer, until it reduces by half, it makes a good pizza-base sauce or, with capers stirred through it, a delicious topping for chicken or veal scaloppine.

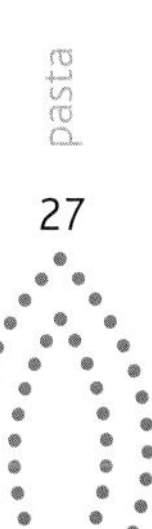

spaghetti puttanesca

PREPARATION TIME 15 MINUTES COOKING TIME 20 MINUTES

- 1/4 cup (60ml) olive oil
- 2 cloves garlic, crushed
- 4 medium tomatoes (760g), chopped coarsely
- 1/2 cup finely chopped fresh parsley
- 12 stuffed olives, sliced thinly
- 45g canned anchovy fillets, chopped finely
- 1 tablespoon finely chopped fresh basil
- pinch chilli powder
- 375g spaghetti

1 Heat oil in medium saucepan; cook garlic until just changed in colour.

2 Add tomato, parsley, olives, anchovy, basil and chilli powder; cook further 3 minutes.

3 Meanwhile, cook pasta in large saucepan of boiling water, uncovered, until just tender; drain.

4 Combine pasta in large warmed bowl, with sauce; toss gently.

SERVES 4

PER SERVING 16.9G FAT; 2055KJ (491 CAL)

spaghetti marinara

PREPARATION TIME 5 MINUTES COOKING TIME 15 MINUTES

1 tablespoon olive oil
1 medium brown onion (150g), chopped finely
1/3 cup (80ml) dry white wine
1/3 cup (95g) tomato paste
850g canned tomatoes
750g seafood marinara mix
1/4 cup loosely packed, coarsely chopped fresh flat-leaf parsley
375g spaghetti

1 Heat oil in large frying pan; cook onion, stirring, until soft.
2 Add wine, paste and undrained crushed tomatoes to pan; bring to a boil. Reduce heat; simmer, uncovered, 10 minutes or until sauce thickens slightly.
3 Add marinara mix; cook, stirring occasionally, about 5 minutes or until seafood is cooked through. Stir in parsley.
4 Meanwhile, cook pasta in large saucepan of boiling water, uncovered, until just tender; drain.
5 Serve marinara over pasta.

SERVES 4
PER SERVING 11.6G FAT; 2820KJ (674 CAL)

spaghetti with pesto

PREPARATION TIME 15 MINUTES COOKING TIME 15 MINUTES

- 2 cups coarsely chopped fresh basil
- 2 tablespoons pine nuts, toasted
- 2 cloves garlic
- 1/3 cup (80ml) olive oil
- 1/4 cup (20g) finely grated parmesan cheese
- 375g spaghetti

1 Blend or process basil, pine nuts and garlic until smooth. With processor operating, add oil in thin stream; process further 1 second.

2 Place basil mixture in medium bowl. Add cheese; mix until combined.

3 Cook pasta in large saucepan of boiling water, uncovered, until just tender; drain.

4 Combine pasta with pesto in large warmed bowl; toss gently.

SERVES 4

PER SERVING 26.5 FAT; 2363KJ (564 CAL)

STORE PESTO CAN BE MADE 2 WEEKS AHEAD AND REFRIGERATED IN STERILISED JAR WITH A THIN LAYER OF OLIVE OIL OVER TOP, OR FROZEN, IN FREEZER CONTAINER, FOR UP TO 3 MONTHS.

spaghetti with herbed ricotta

PREPARATION TIME 10 MINUTES COOKING TIME 15 MINUTES

- 500g spaghetti
- 450g fresh ricotta
- 3 egg yolks
- 3/4 cup (180ml) milk
- 1/3 cup firmly packed, coarsely chopped fresh flat-leaf parsley
- 1/4 cup firmly packed, coarsely chopped fresh basil
- 3 spring onions, chopped finely
- 2 cloves garlic, crushed
- 1/4 cup (20g) finely grated pepato cheese
- freshly ground black pepper

1 Cook pasta in large saucepan of boiling water, uncovered, until just tender; drain.

2 Whisk ricotta, yolks and milk in large bowl until smooth; stir in herbs, onion, garlic and cheese.

3 Add pasta to ricotta mixture; toss gently to combine. Sprinkle with pepper to serve.

SERVES 4

PER SERVING 21.7G FAT; 2863KJ (684 CAL)

TIPS Pepato can be substituted with another hard cheese, such as romano or an aged provolone. Feel free to use other herbs, such as chives or oregano, instead of the basil.

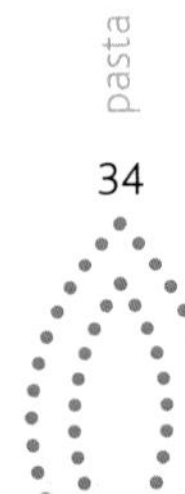

fettuccine carbonara

PREPARATION TIME 10 MINUTES COOKING TIME 10 MINUTES

4 bacon rashers (280g), chopped coarsely
375g fettuccine
3 egg yolks, beaten
1 cup (250ml) cream
1/2 cup (40g) finely grated parmesan cheese
2 tablespoons coarsely chopped fresh chives

1 Cook bacon in small heated frying pan, stirring, until crisp; drain.
2 Just before serving, cook pasta in large saucepan of boiling water, uncovered, until just tender; drain.
3 Combine pasta in warmed large bowl with yolks, cream and cheese; sprinkle with chives and freshly ground black pepper, if desired.

SERVES 4
PER SERVING 42G FAT; 3222KJ (770 CAL)

TIP Pancetta or prosciutto can be substituted for the bacon, and grated romano or pepato can be substituted for the parmesan.

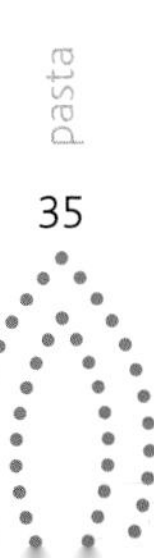

fettuccine with meatballs in rosemary paprika sauce

PREPARATION TIME 15 MINUTES COOKING TIME 45 MINUTES

250g lean minced beef
1/2 cup (35g) stale breadcrumbs
1 tablespoon finely chopped fresh parsley
1 tablespoon finely chopped fresh chives
1 egg white
1 teaspoon worcestershire sauce
2 teaspoons olive oil
250g fettuccine

ROSEMARY PAPRIKA SAUCE
425g canned tomatoes
1 cup (250ml) water
2 tablespoons dry red wine
1 medium brown onion (150g), chopped finely
1/2 teaspoon worcestershire sauce
1 teaspoon sweet paprika
3 sprigs rosemary

1 Combine beef, breadcrumbs, parsley, chives, egg white and sauce in large bowl. Shape mixture into small meatballs.
2 Heat oil in medium non-stick saucepan; cook meatballs until well browned all over and cooked through. Drain on absorbent paper.
3 Meanwhile, cook pasta in large saucepan of boiling water until tender; drain.
4 Add meatballs to rosemary paprika sauce; mix well. Stir until heated through. [Can be made 2 days ahead to this stage and refrigerated, covered, or frozen for up to 3 months.]
5 Serve pasta with meatballs in rosemary paprika sauce.

ROSEMARY PAPRIKA SAUCE Combine undrained crushed tomatoes with remaining ingredients in medium saucepan; bring to a boil. Reduce heat; simmer, uncovered, about 20 minutes or until thickened slightly.

SERVES 2
PER SERVING 15.8G FAT; 3303KJ (789 CAL)

pappardelle with chilli and semi-dried tomato sauce

PREPARATION TIME 15 MINUTES COOKING TIME 25 MINUTES

- 2 medium brown onions (300g), chopped coarsely
- 2 cloves garlic, quartered
- 1 cup (150g) semi-dried tomatoes in oil, drained
- 1/4 cup (70g) tomato paste
- 2 fresh red thai chillies, deseeded, chopped finely
- 2 cups (500ml) beef stock
- 375g pappardelle
- 1/4 cup coarsely chopped fresh flat-leaf parsley
- freshly ground black pepper

1 Blend or process onion, garlic, tomatoes, tomato paste and chilli until mixture forms a paste.
2 Heat large non-stick frying pan; cook tomato mixture, stirring, 10 minutes. Stir in stock; bring to a boil. Reduce heat; simmer sauce, uncovered, about 10 minutes or until thickened slightly. [Can be made 2 days ahead to this stage and refrigerated, covered, or frozen for up to 6 months.]
3 Meanwhile, cook pasta in large saucepan of boiling water, uncovered, until just tender; drain.
4 Just before serving, gently toss pasta through sauce; sprinkle with parsley and pepper.

SERVES 6

PER SERVING 2.9G FAT; 1147KJ (274 CAL)

TIP Pappardelle is the widest ribbon pasta available; any long pasta such as fettuccine or tagliatelle can be substituted.

cheese and spinach tortellini with gorgonzola sauce

PREPARATION TIME 5 MINUTES
COOKING TIME 15 MINUTES

30g butter
2 tablespoons plain flour
1 cup (250ml) milk
3/4 cup (180ml) cream
100g gorgonzola cheese, chopped coarsely
750g cheese and spinach tortellini
1/4 cup loosely packed fresh flat-leaf parsley
freshly ground black pepper

1 Melt butter in medium saucepan; cook flour, stirring, about 2 minutes or until mixture bubbles and thickens.
2 Gradually stir in milk and cream; bring to a boil. Reduce heat; simmer, uncovered, until sauce boils and thickens. Remove from heat; stir in cheese.
3 Meanwhile, cook pasta in large saucepan of boiling water, uncovered, until just tender; drain.
4 Combine pasta with sauce; sprinkle with parsley and pepper.

SERVES 4
PER SERVING 43.8G FAT; 3017KJ (721 CAL)

TIPS Ravioli or gnocchi can be substituted for the tortellini. It's best to choose a ricotta-and-spinach-filled tortellini (or the even simpler ricotta-filled version) when making this sauce, as it doesn't marry overly well with meat-filled pastas.

rigatoni with aubergine sauce

PREPARATION TIME 10 MINUTES COOKING TIME 20 MINUTES

- 1/4 cup (60ml) olive oil
- 1 medium brown onion (150g), chopped finely
- 2 trimmed sticks celery (150g), chopped finely
- 1 clove garlic, crushed
- 2 tablespoons brandy
- 1 medium aubergine (300g), sliced thinly
- 2 1/3 cups (580ml) bottled tomato pasta sauce
- 1/2 cup (140g) tomato paste
- 1/2 cup (125ml) water
- 375g rigatoni
- 1/4 cup (20g) finely grated parmesan cheese

1 Heat oil in large saucepan; cook onion, celery and garlic, stirring, until onion softens. Add brandy; cook, stirring, until brandy evaporates. Add aubergine; cook, stirring, until aubergine is tender.

2 Stir in sauce, paste and the water; bring to a boil. Reduce heat; simmer, uncovered, about 10 minutes or until sauce thickens slightly. [Can be made 2 days ahead to this stage and refrigerated, covered.]

3 Meanwhile, cook pasta in large saucepan of boiling water, uncovered, until just tender; drain. Place pasta in large warmed bowl with half of the aubergine sauce; toss gently to combine. Divide pasta among serving plates; top each with remaining sauce. Serve with cheese.

SERVES 4

PER SERVING 16.9G FAT; 2420KJ (578 CAL)

TIP Before serving, warm large bowls and platters, by placing in a sink of very hot water 10 minutes; dry before using.

lasagne

PREPARATION TIME 40 MINUTES COOKING TIME 2 HOURS 10 MINUTES

1 tablespoon olive oil
1 medium onion (150g), chopped finely
1 medium carrot (120g), chopped finely
1 trimmed stick celery (75g), chopped finely
2 cloves garlic, crushed
500g minced beef
1/3 cup (80ml) dry red wine
850g canned tomatoes
2 tablespoons tomato paste
1/2 cup (125ml) water
4 slices prosciutto (60g), chopped finely
1 tablespoon coarsely chopped fresh oregano
2 tablespoons coarsely chopped fresh parsley
18 instant lasagne sheets
1/2 cup (40g) grated parmesan cheese

CHEESE SAUCE
60g butter
1/3 cup (50g) plain flour
1 litre (4 cups) milk
3/4 cup (60g) grated parmesan cheese
pinch ground nutmeg

1 Heat oil in large frying pan; cook onion, carrot, celery and garlic, stirring, until onion is soft. Add beef; cook, stirring, until browned. Add wine; bring to a boil. Stir in undrained crushed tomatoes, paste and the water; reduce heat. Simmer, uncovered, about 1 hour or until mixture is thick. Stir in prosciutto and herbs; cool slightly.
2 Place six lasagne sheets into greased shallow 3-litre (12 cup) ovenproof dish. Spread with half of the meat sauce; drizzle with 1 cup (250ml) of the cheese sauce. Repeat layers again.
3 Top with remaining pasta sheets. Spread with remaining cheese sauce; sprinkle with cheese. Bake in moderate oven about 45 minutes or until pasta is tender and lasagne is browned.

CHEESE SAUCE Heat butter in large saucepan; cook flour, stirring over heat until flour bubbles and thickens. Remove from heat; gradually stir in milk. Cook, until mixture boils and thickens. Remove from heat; stir in cheese and nutmeg. Cool 10 minutes.

SERVES 6
PER SERVING 32.4G FAT; 2934KJ (701 CAL)
STORE RECIPE BEST MADE A DAY AHEAD; CAN BE MADE 3 DAYS AHEAD AND REFRIGERATED, COVERED, OR FROZEN FOR UP TO 2 MONTHS.

pasta primavera

PREPARATION TIME 15 MINUTES COOKING TIME 15 MINUTES

- 375g small spiral pasta
- 1 tablespoon olive oil
- 1 medium brown onion (150g), chopped finely
- 3 cloves garlic, crushed
- 300g yellow patty-pan squash, quartered
- 1 medium red pepper (200g), sliced thinly
- 200g sugar snap peas
- 1 medium carrot (120g), cut into ribbons
- 1¼ cups (310ml) cream
- 1 tablespoon seeded mustard
- 2 tablespoons finely chopped fresh flat-leaf parsley

1 Cook pasta in large saucepan of boiling water, uncovered, until just tender; drain.

2 Meanwhile, heat oil in large saucepan; cook onion and garlic, stirring, until onion softens. Add squash; cook, stirring, until just tender. Add capsicum, peas and carrot; cook, stirring, until capsicum is just tender.

3 Place pasta in pan with vegetables; add combined remaining ingredients. Stir over low heat until just hot.

SERVES 4

PER SERVING 38.9G FAT; 3033KJ (724 CAL)

penne arrabiata

PREPARATION TIME 10 MINUTES
COOKING TIME 15 MINUTES

1 tablespoon olive oil
2 medium brown onions (300g), chopped finely
5 cloves garlic, crushed
3 fresh red thai chillies, chopped finely
2 1/3 cups (580ml) bottled tomato pasta sauce
2 teaspoons balsamic vinegar
375g penne
1/4 cup (20g) finely grated parmesan cheese

1 Heat oil in large saucepan; cook onion, garlic and chilli, stirring, until onion softens. Add sauce and vinegar; bring to a boil. Reduce heat; simmer, uncovered, about 5 minutes or until sauce thickens slightly. [Can be made a day ahead to this stage and refrigerated, covered, or frozen for up to 6 months.]

2 Meanwhile, cook pasta in large saucepan of boiling water, uncovered, until just tender; drain. Combine pasta with sauce; sprinkle with cheese.

SERVES 4
PER SERVING 7.6G FAT; 1904KJ (455 CAL)

TIP Leftover pasta and sauce can be placed in an oiled ovenproof dish, covered with mozzarella and baked in moderate oven until heated through and cheese bubbles.

roasted tomato, goat's cheese and chicken pizza

PREPARATION TIME 25 MINUTES COOKING TIME 35 MINUTES

500g cherry tomatoes, halved
2 tablespoons balsamic vinegar
2 tablespoons brown sugar
2 chicken breast fillets (340g)
30cm round homemade or purchased pizza base
2 tablespoons coarsely chopped fresh coriander
80g goat's cheese
40g rocket

1 Place tomatoes on oven tray lined with baking parchment; drizzle with combined vinegar and sugar. Bake, uncovered, in very hot oven about 25 minutes or until tomatoes are soft.
2 Meanwhile, cook chicken on heated oiled griddle (or grill or barbecue) until browned both sides and cooked through. Cool 5 minutes; cut into thin slices. Place pizza base on oven tray; bake, uncovered, in hot oven about 10 minutes or until browned lightly.
3 Top pizza with tomato, chicken, coriander and crumbled cheese. Bake, uncovered, in very hot oven, 10 minutes or until pizza is browned and crisp.
4 Just before serving, top with rocket.

SERVES 2
PER SERVING 17.6G FAT; 3278KJ (783 CAL)

TIP Using baking parchment will prevent the skin of the tomatoes sticking to the oven tray.

swiss chard and fetta pizza

PREPARATION TIME 25 MINUTES (PLUS STANDING TIME)
COOKING TIME 30 MINUTES

2 teaspoons (7g) dry yeast
1 teaspoon sugar
2½ cups (375g) plain flour
1 cup (250ml) warm water
½ teaspoon salt
2 tablespoons olive oil
¼ cup (40g) semolina
500g swiss chard
1 cup (200g) crumbled fetta cheese
⅓ cup (25g) finely grated parmesan cheese
10 cherry tomatoes (100g), halved

TOMATO SAUCE
1 tablespoon olive oil
1 medium brown onion (150g), chopped coarsely
2 cloves garlic, crushed
425g canned tomatoes
½ cup (140g) tomato paste
¼ cup coarsely chopped fresh basil
1 teaspoon sugar

1 Combine yeast, sugar, 1 tablespoon of the flour and the water in small bowl; whisk until yeast dissolves. Cover; stand in warm place about 10 minutes or until mixture is frothy.
2 Combine remaining sifted flour and salt in processor; pour in combined yeast mixture and oil while motor is operating. Process until dough forms a ball. Turn dough onto floured surface; knead 10 minutes or until dough is smooth and elastic. Place dough in oiled large bowl. Cover; stand in warm place about 30 minutes or until dough doubles in size.
3 Turn dough onto surface sprinkled with half of the semolina; knead 1 minute. Place dough on oiled large oven tray sprinkled with remaining semolina; press dough into a 32cm square.
4 Boil, steam or microwave swiss chard until wilted. Drain; cool. Squeeze as much liquid as possible from swiss chard; chop finely. Spread pizza base with tomato sauce. Spread evenly with swiss chard, cheeses and tomato. Bake in very hot oven about 20 minutes.

TOMATO SAUCE Heat oil in medium saucepan; cook onion and garlic, stirring, until onion is soft. Stir in undrained crushed tomatoes, paste, basil and sugar; simmer, uncovered, about 5 minutes or until thickened.

SERVES 6
PER SERVING 19.5G FAT; 2022KJ (483 CAL)

pepperoni pizza in a flash

PREPARATION TIME 10 MINUTES COOKING TIME 20 MINUTES

30cm homemade or purchased pizza base
1/3 cup (90g) tomato paste
2 teaspoons dried oregano
2 cups (200g) grated mozzarella cheese
1/4 cup (20g) grated parmesan cheese
150g sliced pepperoni
1/2 cup (80g) pitted black olives

1 Place pizza base on oiled pizza tray. Spread base with combined tomato paste and oregano; sprinkle with two-thirds of the combined cheeses. Top with pepperoni and olives, then remaining cheeses.
2 Bake, uncovered, in moderately hot oven about 20 minutes or until base is cooked through and cheese is bubbling.

SERVES 4
PER SERVING 29G FAT; 2311KJ (552 CAL)

TIP Any salami, cabanossi or ham can be substituted for the pepperoni.

marinara pizza

PREPARATION TIME 25 MINUTES COOKING TIME 40 MINUTES

- 250g medium uncooked prawns
- 250g marinara seafood mix
- 1 tablespoon olive oil
- 1 medium white onion (150g), chopped finely
- 1 clove garlic, crushed
- 425g canned tomatoes
- 1/3 cup (80ml) dry white wine
- 30cm homemade or purchased pizza base
- 3 cloves garlic, crushed, extra
- 1/4 cup (70g) tomato paste
- 2 teaspoons dried oregano

1 Peel and devein prawns. Rinse marinara mix under cold running water; drain well.

2 Heat oil in large frying pan; cook onion and garlic, stirring, until onion is soft. Add undrained crushed tomatoes and wine. Simmer, uncovered, until sauce thickens.

3 Add seafood; simmer, uncovered, 2 minutes or until seafood just changes colour. Remove seafood with slotted spoon. Continue simmering sauce until very thick.

4 Place pizza base on oiled pizza tray. Spread with combined garlic, paste and oregano. Spoon seafood, then sauce over pizza.

5 Bake, uncovered, in moderately hot oven about 20 minutes or until base is cooked though and seafood is tender.

SERVES 4

PER SERVING 9.5G FAT: 1601KJ (382 CAL)

TIP If you prefer to use just prawns for this pizza, you will need 750g medium uncooked prawns.

tomato and onion pitta pizzas

PREPARATION TIME 15 MINUTES COOKING TIME 15 MINUTES

- 4 wholemeal pittas
- 1/4 cup (60ml) bottled tomato pasta sauce
- 1 cup (125g) grated cheddar cheese
- 2 medium tomatoes (380g), sliced thinly
- 1 medium brown onion (150g), sliced thinly
- 1/4 cup (30g) pitted black olives, halved

1 Place pitta in single layer on lightly oiled oven tray. Spread each pitta with pasta sauce; top with half of the cheese. Top with tomato, onion and olives; sprinkle with remaining cheese.

2 Bake pizzas in hot oven about 15 minutes or until browned lightly.

SERVES 4

PER SERVING 16.7G FAT; 1633KJ (390 CAL)

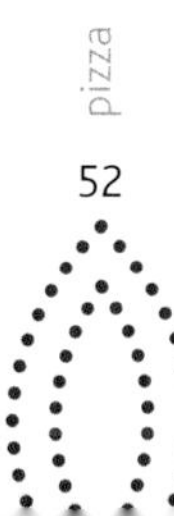

pesto, bocconcini and artichoke pizza

PREPARATION TIME 10 MINUTES COOKING TIME 25 MINUTES

30cm homemade or purchased pizza base
190g jar pesto
100g marinated aubergine slices
200g char-grilled pepper slices
2 drained marinated artichoke hearts, sliced thickly
6 bocconcini cheeses (200g), sliced thickly
2 tablespoons pine nuts

1 Place pizza base on oiled pizza tray. Spread pesto over base; top with aubergine, pepper and artichokes. Arrange bocconcini on top; sprinkle with pine nuts.
2 Bake, uncovered, in moderately hot oven about 20 minutes or until base is cooked through and cheese is bubbling.

SERVES 4
PER SERVING 40.1G FAT; 2581KJ (616 CAL)

TIP The same amount of ingredients used to top a 30cm pizza will top four mini pizza bases.

salami, mushroom and oregano pizza

PREPARATION TIME 15 MINUTES COOKING TIME 20 MINUTES

- 30cm homemade or purchased pizza base
- 1/4 cup (70g) tomato paste
- 2 teaspoons dried oregano
- 1/3 cup (80ml) bottled tomato pasta sauce
- 1/2 cup (150g) coarsely chopped cooked swiss chard
- 50g button mushrooms, sliced thinly
- 100g sliced salami
- 3/4 cup (75g) grated mozzarella cheese

1 Place pizza base on lightly oiled pizza tray. Spread combined tomato paste and oregano over pizza base. Top with pasta sauce, swiss chard, mushrooms, then salami. Sprinkle with cheese.

2 Bake, uncovered, in moderately hot oven, about 20 minutes or until base is cooked through and cheese is bubbling.

SERVES 4

PER SERVING 16.5G FAT; 1596KJ (381 CAL)

TIPS Split a purchased base in half for a thin crust pizza. Use cut-side up and bake about 5 minutes less than the time stated. Use your choice of mild or hot salami for this pizza.

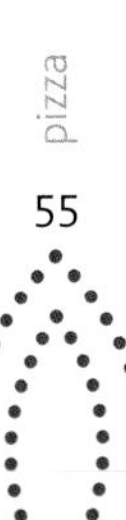

pizza with prosciutto and ricotta

PREPARATION TIME 15 MINUTES COOKING TIME 15 MINUTES

3 medium plum tomatoes (225g)
3 x 25cm homemade or purchased pizza bases
1/2 cup (140g) tomato paste
300g baby spinach
1 large red onion (300g), sliced thinly
9 slices prosciutto (135g), halved
1/4 cup loosely packed, coarsely chopped fresh basil
1 1/2 cups (300g) ricotta cheese
1/4 cup (40g) pine nuts
1/4 cup (60ml) olive oil
2 cloves garlic, crushed

1 Cut each tomato into eight wedges.
2 Place pizza bases on oven trays. Spread each base with a third of the tomato paste; top with equal amounts of tomato, spinach, onion, prosciutto, basil, cheese and pine nuts. Drizzle each pizza with equal amounts of combined oil and garlic.
3 Bake, uncovered, in very hot oven about 15 minutes or until pizza tops are browned lightly and bases are crisp.

SERVES 6
PER SERVING 27.6G FAT; 2934KJ (701 CAL)

vegetarian calzone

PREPARATION TIME 40 MINUTES (PLUS STANDING TIME)
COOKING TIME 50 MINUTES

2 teaspoons (7g) dried yeast
1 teaspoon sugar
1½ cups (375ml) warm water
4 cups (600g) plain flour
1 teaspoon salt
½ teaspoon cracked black pepper
2 tablespoons olive oil
1 cup (125g) coarsely grated cheddar cheese

VEGETABLE FILLING
1 small aubergine (230g), chopped coarsely
coarse cooking salt
1 tablespoon olive oil
1 large brown onion (200g), chopped coarsely
2 cloves garlic, crushed
1 medium red pepper (200g), chopped coarsely
2 medium courgettes (240g), chopped coarsely
2 trimmed sticks celery (150g), chopped coarsely
2 tablespoons tomato paste
½ cup (125ml) vegetable stock

1 Whisk yeast, sugar and the water together in small bowl. Cover; stand in warm place about 10 minutes or until mixture is frothy.
2 Place flour, salt and pepper in large bowl. Stir in yeast mixture and oil; mix to a firm dough. Turn dough onto floured surface; knead about 10 minutes or until smooth and elastic. Place dough in large oiled bowl. Cover; stand in warm place about 30 minutes or until doubled in size.
3 Transfer dough to floured surface; knead until smooth. Divide dough into four pieces; roll each piece to a 24cm round. Spread one half of each round with a quarter of the vegetable filling; top with a quarter of the cheese. Fold plain dough over cheese to enclose filling; press edges together.
4 Place calzone on oiled oven trays; brush with a little extra oil. Cut two small slits on top of each calzone; bake, uncovered, in hot oven about 20 minutes or until browned.

VEGETABLE FILLING Place aubergine in strainer. Sprinkle with salt; stand 30 minutes. Rinse aubergine under cold running water; drain on absorbent paper. Heat oil in large frying pan; cook onion and garlic, stirring, until onion is soft. Add aubergine, pepper, courgette and celery; cook, stirring, about 5 minutes or until vegetables are soft. Add paste and stock. Cook, stirring, until mixture thickens; cool. [Can be made a day ahead to this stage and refrigerated, covered, or frozen for up to 2 months.]

SERVES 4
PER SERVING 26.8G FAT; 3497KJ (835 CAL)

roasted squash and rosemary risotto

PREPARATION TIME 20 MINUTES COOKING TIME 40 MINUTES

- 1kg butternut squash, chopped coarsely
- 1/4 cup (60ml) olive oil
- 1 1/2 cups (300g) arborio rice
- 1 clove garlic, crushed
- 1 tablespoon fresh rosemary
- 1 litre (4 cups) hot vegetable stock
- 150g baby spinach
- 1/4 cup (20g) coarsely grated parmesan cheese
- 1/4 cup (60ml) cream
- 2 tablespoons parmesan cheese flakes

1 Combine squash and half of the oil in baking dish. Bake, uncovered, in moderate oven, about 40 minutes or until squash is tender.
2 Meanwhile, heat remaining oil in large saucepan. Add rice; stir to coat in oil. Add garlic and rosemary; cook, stirring, until fragrant.
3 Stir in 1 cup of the stock; cook, stirring, over low heat until liquid is absorbed.
4 Continue adding stock, in 1-cup batches, stirring after each addition. Total cooking time should be about 35 minutes or until rice is tender; remove from heat.
5 Stir in squash, spinach, grated parmesan and cream. Stir over heat until hot. Serve topped with parmesan flakes.

SERVES 4
PER SERVING 25.3G FAT; 2484KJ (593 CAL)

TIP Leftover risotto can be made into patties and pan-fried. Serve topped with crisp prosciutto; dot with sour cream.

lemon risotto

PREPARATION TIME 15 MINUTES COOKING TIME 40 MINUTES

- 4 cups (1 litre) chicken stock
- 1 cup (250ml) dry white wine
- 2 teaspoons finely grated lemon rind
- 1 tablespoon lemon juice
- 80g butter
- 1 medium brown onion (150g), chopped finely
- 2 cups (400g) arborio rice
- 3/4 cup (60g) finely grated parmesan cheese
- 2 tablespoons finely chopped fresh flat-leaf parsley
- 1 medium lemon (140g), quartered

1 Bring stock and wine to a boil in medium saucepan. Add rind and juice; reduce heat. Cover; keep hot.
2 Heat half of the butter in large saucepan; cook onion, stirring, until soft. Add rice; stir over medium heat until coated in butter mixture.
3 Stir 1 cup of the stock mixture into rice mixture; cook, stirring, over low heat until liquid is absorbed.
4 Continue adding stock mixture in 1-cup batches, stirring after each addition. Total cooking time should be about 35 minutes.
5 Remove pan from heat; serve topped with cheese and parsley. Accompany risotto with lemon quarters.

SERVES 4
PER SERVING 22.1G FAT; 2805KJ (670 CAL)

risotto milanese

PREPARATION TIME 15 MINUTES COOKING TIME 40 MINUTES

3 1/2 cups (875ml) hot chicken stock
1/2 cup (125ml) dry white wine
1/4 teaspoon saffron
50g butter
1 large brown onion (200g), chopped finely
1 3/4 cups (350g) arborio rice
2 tablespoons grated parmesan cheese

1 Bring stock, wine and saffron to a boil in medium saucepan. Reduce heat; simmer, covered, while preparing onion and rice.
2 Heat half of the butter in large saucepan; cook onion, stirring until soft. Add rice; stir over medium heat until coated in butter mixture. Stir in 1 cup (250ml) of the stock mixture; cook, stirring, over low heat until liquid is absorbed.
3 Continue adding stock mixture in 1-cup batches, stirring after each addition until liquid is absorbed. Total cooking time should be about 35 minutes or until rice is tender.
4 Stir in remaining butter and cheese.

SERVES 2
PER SERVING 25.5G FAT; 3970KJ (948 CAL)

buttery wine risotto with smoked salmon

PREPARATION TIME 10 MINUTES COOKING TIME 40 MINUTES

6 cups (1.5 litres) chicken stock
1 cup (250ml) dry white wine
40g butter
1 medium leek (350g), chopped finely
2 cloves garlic, crushed
2 cups (400g) arborio rice
1/4 teaspoon ground turmeric
40g butter, chopped finely, extra
1/2 cup (40g) finely grated parmesan cheese
100g smoked salmon, chopped coarsely
2 teaspoons finely chopped fresh dill
50g baby spinach

1 Bring stock and wine to a boil in medium saucepan; reduce heat. Cover; keep hot.

2 Heat butter in large saucepan; cook leek and garlic, stirring, until leek is very soft. Add rice and turmeric; stir to coat in butter mixture. Stir in 1 cup of the stock mixture; cook, stirring, over low heat until liquid is absorbed.

3 Continue adding stock mixture in 1-cup batches, stirring after each addition. Total cooking time should be about 35 minutes or until rice is tender. Remove pan from heat; stir in extra butter, cheese, salmon, dill and spinach.

SERVES 4
PER SERVING 23.1G FAT; 2824KJ (675 CAL)

gnocchi with burnt butter and sage

PREPARATION TIME 25 MINUTES (PLUS REFRIGERATION TIME)
COOKING TIME 25 MINUTES

3 large desiree potatoes (900g)
1 clove garlic, crushed
2 tablespoons milk
2 egg yolks
1/3 cup (25g) grated parmesan cheese
1 cup (150g) plain flour, approximately
125g butter, chopped coarsely
12 fresh sage leaves
1/4 cup (20g) parmesan cheese flakes, extra
freshly ground black pepper

1 Steam or boil whole unpeeled potatoes until tender; drain. Cool potatoes slightly; peel. Mash potatoes with a ricer, mouli or masher until smooth; stir in garlic and milk. Stir in egg yolks, grated parmesan and enough of the flour to form a firm dough.

2 Roll a quarter of the dough on lightly floured surface into a 2cm-thick sausage. Cut into 2cm lengths; roll into gnocchi-shaped ovals. Place each oval in palm of hand; press with inverted floured fork tines to flatten gnocchi slightly and make a grooved imprint. Place on lightly floured tray in single layer. Cover; refrigerate 1 hour. [Can be made a day ahead to this stage and refrigerated, covered, or frozen for up to 3 months.]

3 Cook gnocchi, in batches, in large saucepan of boiling water about 3 minutes or until gnocchi float to the surface. Remove from pan with slotted spoon; drain.

4 Meanwhile, cook butter in small shallow frying pan until just browned. Add sage; immediately remove from heat. Divide gnocchi among serving plates; drizzle with sage butter. Serve topped with parmesan flakes and pepper.

SERVES 4
PER SERVING 33.2G FAT; 2483KJ (593 CAL)

TIP A ricer or mouli, available from kitchenware stores, will give the best result for smooth potato.

spinach gnocchi

PREPARATION TIME 30 MINUTES COOKING TIME 20 MINUTES

500g spinach
$1\frac{1}{4}$ cups (250g) ricotta cheese
1 cup (80g) finely grated parmesan cheese
1 egg, beaten lightly
$\frac{1}{4}$ teaspoon ground nutmeg
plain flour
45g butter, melted

1 Steam or microwave spinach until wilted. Rinse under cold running water; drain well. Squeeze as much liquid as possible from spinach; chop finely.
2 Combine spinach, ricotta, half of the parmesan, egg and nutmeg in medium bowl.
3 Using tablespoon and palm of hand, roll mixture into egg shapes.
4 Roll gnocchi lightly in flour. Cook gnocchi, in batches, in large saucepan of boiling water, uncovered, about 3 minutes or until gnocchi float to the surface. Remove from pan with slotted spoon; drain.
5 Arrange gnocchi in ovenproof dish. Pour butter over gnocchi; sprinkle with remaining parmesan. [Can be made a day ahead to this stage and refrigerated, covered; reheat in moderate oven about 20 minutes or until hot.] Cook under moderately hot grill until cheese turns golden brown.

SERVES 4
PER SERVING 25.1G FAT; 1376KJ (329 CAL)

gnocchi alla romana

PREPARATION TIME 30 MINUTES (PLUS REFRIGERATING TIME)
COOKING TIME 40 MINUTES

3 cups (750ml) milk
$1\frac{1}{2}$ teaspoons salt
pinch ground nutmeg
$\frac{2}{3}$ cup (110g) semolina
1 egg, beaten lightly
$1\frac{1}{2}$ cups (120g) grated parmesan cheese
60g butter, melted

1 Bring milk, salt and nutmeg to a boil in medium saucepan; reduce heat. Gradually add semolina, stirring constantly with wooden spoon.
2 Continue cooking, uncovered, stirring often, about 10 minutes, or until spoon can stand upright in centre. Remove from heat.
3 Combine egg and 1 cup (80g) of the cheese in small bowl. Add to semolina mixture; stir well. Spread mixture onto well-oiled 26cm x 32cm swiss roll tin; using wet spatula smooth until 5mm thick. Refrigerate about 1 hour or until semolina is firm.
4 Cut semolina into circles using 4cm pastry cutter. Arrange circles, overlapping, in greased shallow ovenproof dish. Pour over butter; sprinkle with remaining cheese. Bake in moderate oven about 15 minutes or until crisp and golden.

SERVES 4
PER SERVING 31.4G FAT; 2009KJ (480 CAL)

polenta

PREPARATION TIME 15 MINUTES (PLUS STANDING TIME)
COOKING TIME 50 MINUTES

This is a specialty of northern Italy, particularly popular around Venice. Served plain, it is often accompanied by bolognese sauce; or it can be fried and served as an accompaniment to any meat. Hot, fried polenta can also be topped with anchovies and sliced olives or other toppings and served as crostini.

- 8 cups (2 litres) water
- 2 teaspoons salt
- 2 cups (340g) polenta
- 1/4 cup (60ml) olive oil

1 Combine the water and salt in large saucepan; bring to a boil. Gradually sprinkle polenta over the water, stirring constantly with wooden spoon; make sure polenta has no lumps.

2 Reduce heat to low, as mixture may bubble and spatter; partially covering the saucepan is a good idea. Continue cooking, stirring, about 30 minutes or until polenta is very thick and spoon can stand upright in centre. [Polenta can be served at this point, piled onto a plate.]

3 Spoon mixture into greased 20cm x 30cm baking tin; spread mixture out evenly. Allow to become cold; leave at room temperature a few hours.

4 Turn polenta out of pan; cut into 4cm slices. Heat oil in large frying pan until very hot; reduce heat. Gently fry polenta slices until golden brown both sides.

SERVES 4
PER SERVING 15.4G FAT; 1678KJ (401 CAL)

garlic marinated prawns

PREPARATION TIME 30 MINUTES (PLUS REFRIGERATION TIME)
COOKING TIME 10 MINUTES

1 kg uncooked king prawns
3/4 cup (50g) stale breadcrumbs
6 cloves garlic, crushed
1/2 cup (125ml) olive oil
freshly ground black pepper
1/4 cup (60ml) lemon juice

1 Remove heads from prawns. Using sharp scissors, cut though shells from head to tail, leaving shells intact. Remove vein from prawns.
2 Combine breadcrumbs, garlic, oil and enough of the pepper to season, in large bowl. Add prawns; rub in breadcrumb mixture, trying to get breadcrumbs under shells if possible. Cover; refrigerate 1 hour. [Can be made a day ahead to this stage.]
3 Cook prawns, in batches, on heated oiled griddle (or grill or barbecue), until just cooked through. Sprinkle with juice just before serving.

SERVES 4
PER SERVING 39.8G FAT; 1743KJ (416 CAL)

steamed garlic and herb mussels

PREPARATION TIME 30 MINUTES COOKING TIME 25 MINUTES

80 medium black mussels (approximately 2kg)
2 tablespoons olive oil
8 cloves garlic, crushed
4 fresh red thai chillies, deseeded, chopped finely
1 tablespoon finely grated lemon rind
1 cup (250ml) lemon juice
1 cup (250ml) dry white wine
1/2 cup finely chopped fresh flat-leaf parsley
1/3 cup finely chopped fresh basil

1 Scrub mussels; remove beards.
2 Heat oil in large saucepan; cook garlic, chilli and rind, stirring, about 2 minutes or until fragrant. Add mussels, juice and wine; bring to a boil. Cook, covered, about 5 minutes or until mussels open (discard any that do not open). Remove mussels from pan.
3 Bring pan liquid to a boil; cook, uncovered, about 10 minutes or until mixture thickens slightly. Stir in parsley and basil.
4 Return mussels to pan; simmer, stirring, until heated through.

SERVES 6
PER SERVING 5.9G FAT; 514KJ (123 CAL)

clams with tomato dressing

PREPARATION TIME 30 MINUTES
COOKING TIME 10 MINUTES

2.5kg clams, scrubbed
1/2 cup (125ml) dry white wine
1 small red onion (100g), chopped finely
2 cloves garlic, crushed
2 tablespoons lemon juice
2 tablespoons white wine vinegar
1/2 cup (125ml) olive oil
5 large tomatoes (1.25kg), chopped coarsely
4 spring onions, sliced thinly
2 tablespoons coarsely chopped fresh coriander

1 Rinse clams under cold running water; drain. Place clams in large saucepan with wine. Cover; bring to a boil. Reduce heat; simmer about 5 minutes or until shells open (discard any clams that do not open).
2 Meanwhile, heat large oiled saucepan; cook red onion and garlic over medium heat until browned lightly. Add combined juice, vinegar and oil; cook, stirring, about 2 minutes or until thickened slightly.
3 Drain clams; discard liquid.
4 Gently toss clams with tomato, spring onion, coriander and red onion mixture.

SERVES 4
PER SERVING 30.7G FAT; 1584KJ (378 CAL)

walnut gremolata fish

PREPARATION TIME 25 MINUTES
COOKING TIME 30 MINUTES

$^{1}/_{3}$ cup (35g) walnut pieces, toasted, chopped finely
2 tablespoons finely chopped lemon rind
$^{1}/_{4}$ cup finely chopped fresh parsley
2 cloves garlic, crushed
4 medium potatoes (800g), quartered
40g butter, chopped coarsely
$^{1}/_{4}$ cup (60ml) milk
4 firm white fish fillets (640g)
1 tablespoon olive oil

1 Combine nuts, rind, parsley and half of the garlic in small bowl; cover gremolata.
2 Boil, steam or microwave potato until tender; drain. Mash potato with butter, milk and remaining garlic; keep warm.
3 Meanwhile, brush fish with oil; cook, skin-side down first, on heated oiled grill plate (or grill or barbecue) until browned both sides and cooked through.
4 Serve fish with garlic mash; top with gremolata.

SERVES 4
PER SERVING 24.9G FAT; 1964KJ (469 CAL)

TIP We used bream fillets for this recipe, but any firm white fish fillets are suitable.

fish milanese

PREPARATION TIME 20 MINUTES (PLUS MARINATING TIME)
COOKING TIME 10 MINUTES

1 small brown onion (80g), chopped finely
2 tablespoons lemon juice
1/3 cup (80ml) olive oil
4 fish fillets
plain flour
2 eggs, beaten lightly
1 tablespoon milk
1 cup (100g) packaged breadcrumbs
1 tablespoon olive oil, extra
120g butter
1 clove garlic, crushed
2 teaspoons finely chopped fresh parsley

1 Combine onion, juice and oil in medium shallow bowl; mix well. Add fish; spoon mixture over fish to coat thoroughly. Cover; refrigerate 1 hour, turning occasionally.
2 Remove fish from marinade. Coat lightly with flour; shake away excess. Combine egg and milk in small bowl; dip fish into egg mixture. Coat in breadcrumbs; press on firmly. [Can be made 3 hours ahead to this stage and refrigerated, covered.]
3 Heat extra oil and half of the butter in large frying pan. Cook fish about 3 minutes each side, or until cooked through; drain on absorbent paper.
4 Heat remaining butter in small saucepan. Cook garlic until butter turns light golden brown; add parsley. Pour browned butter over fish.

SERVES 4
PER SERVING 52.4G FAT; 2602KJ (621 CAL)

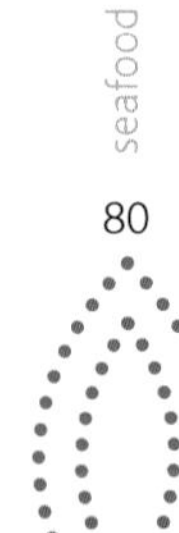

sardines with tomatoes and caper dressing

PREPARATION TIME 20 MINUTES COOKING TIME 10 MINUTES

16 fresh sardines (750g), cleaned
4 medium plum tomatoes (300g), sliced thickly
1 small red onion (100g), sliced thinly
1 tablespoon coarsely chopped fresh flat-leaf parsley

CAPER DRESSING
1/3 cup (80ml) red wine vinegar
1/4 cup (60ml) extra virgin olive oil
1 tablespoon drained baby capers
1 clove garlic, crushed
1 tablespoon finely chopped fresh parsley

1 To butterfly the sardines, cut through the underside of the fish to the tail. Break backbone at tail; peel away backbone. Trim sardines.
2 Cook sardines on heated, oiled griddle (or grill or barbecue), in batches, until browned both sides and just cooked through. Serve with tomato and onion. Spoon over caper dressing; top with parsley.

CAPER DRESSING Combine ingredients in screw-top jar; shake well.

SERVES 4
PER SERVING 33.9G FAT; 2039KJ (487 CAL)

TIP Have sardines cleaned and the heads removed at the fishmonger; they may even butterfly them for you.

calamari

PREPARATION TIME 15 MINUTES COOKING TIME 15 MINUTES

1 egg
2 tablespoons milk
1kg calamari rings, sliced thinly
2 cups (200g) packaged breadcrumbs
vegetable oil for deep-frying

1 Beat egg and milk in small bowl. Dip calamari in egg mixture; drain away excess. Toss in breadcrumbs; press breadcrumbs on firmly. [Can be made 3 hours ahead to this stage and refrigerated, covered.]
2 Heat oil in large saucepan. Deep-fry calamari, in batches, about 2 minutes or until golden brown; drain on absorbent paper. Serve with lemon wedges and tartare sauce, if desired.

SERVES 4
PER SERVING 19.2G FAT; 1474KJ (352 CAL)

TIPS Two cloves of crushed garlic can be added to the egg mixture. Calamari can be shallow-fried. Heat a small amount of oil in large frying pan; the oil should reach only halfway up the side of each calamari ring. Cook calamari rings in hot oil, about 2 minutes each side, or until golden brown.

fritto misto

PREPARATION TIME 35 MINUTES COOKING TIME 20 MINUTES

500g uncooked king prawns
500g small squid
250g white fish fillets
vegetable oil for deep-frying
250g scallops

BATTER
1 cup (150g) self-raising flour
1/4 teaspoon bicarbonate of soda
pinch salt
1 cup (250ml) water, approximately

1 Shell and devein prawns, leaving tails intact. Clean squid; cut into thin rings. Cut fish into 5cm pieces.
2 Heat oil in large saucepan. Dip prawns, squid, fish and scallops into batter; drain off excess. Deep-fry seafood in hot oil, in batches, until golden brown. Drain on absorbent paper. Serve hot with tartare sauce, if desired.

BATTER Combine flour, soda and salt in small bowl. Gradually add the water, stirring until batter is smooth. If batter is too thick, add a little more water.

SERVES 6
PER SERVING 17.6G FAT; 1127KJ (269 CAL)

osso buco

Meaning 'hollow bones', osso buco is served throughout Italy but is a specialty of Milan.

PREPARATION TIME 30 MINUTES COOKING TIME 2 HOURS

- 90g butter
- 2 medium carrots (240g), chopped finely
- 2 large brown onions (400g), chopped finely
- 3 trimmed sticks celery (225g), chopped finely
- 2 cloves garlic, crushed
- 16 pieces veal shin or osso buco (2kg)
- plain flour
- 2 tablespoons olive oil
- 820g canned tomatoes
- 1/2 cup (125ml) dry red wine
- 1 3/4 cups (430ml) beef stock
- 1 tablespoon finely chopped fresh basil
- 1 teaspoon finely chopped fresh thyme
- 1 bay leaf
- 2.5cm strip lemon rind
- 1/4 cup finely chopped fresh parsley
- 1 teaspoon grated lemon rind

1 Heat a third of the butter (30g) in large saucepan; cook carrot, onion, celery and half of the garlic until onion is golden brown. Remove from heat; transfer vegetables to large ovenproof dish.
2 Coat veal with flour. Heat remaining butter and oil in pan. Add veal; brown well each side. Carefully pack veal on top of vegetables.
3 Drain away fat from pan. Add undrained crushed tomatoes, wine, stock, basil, thyme, bay leaf and strip of lemon rind; bring sauce to a boil.
4 Pour sauce over veal. Cover casserole; bake in moderate oven about 1 1/2 hours or until veal is very tender, stirring occasionally. To serve, sprinkle with combined remaining garlic, parsley and grated lemon rind.

SERVES 6
PER SERVING 9.6G FAT; 1695KJ (405 CAL)

TIP The traditional accompaniment for osso buco is risotto milanese (page 63).

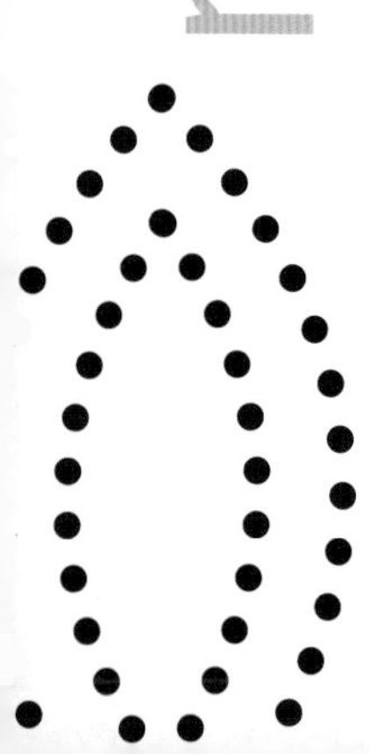

veal parmesan

PREPARATION TIME 35 MINUTES COOKING TIME 1 HOUR 20 MINUTES

4 veal steaks (320g)
plain flour
1 egg
1 tablespoon water
packaged breadcrumbs
30g butter
1/3 cup (80ml) olive oil
2 1/2 cups (250g) grated mozzarella cheese
3/4 cup (60g) grated parmesan cheese

TOMATO SAUCE
1 tablespoon olive oil
1 medium brown onion (150g), chopped finely
1 trimmed stick celery (75g), chopped finely
1 medium red pepper (200g), chopped finely
1 clove garlic, crushed
410g canned tomatoes
2 teaspoons sugar
1 tablespoon tomato paste
1 1/2 cups (375ml) chicken stock
1 tablespoon finely chopped fresh parsley
1 tablespoon finely chopped fresh basil

1 Pound veal out thinly. Toss veal in flour; shake off excess. Dip in combined beaten egg and water; press on breadcrumbs. Refrigerate veal while preparing tomato sauce.

2 Heat butter and half of the oil in large frying pan; cook veal until browned both sides. Place in ovenproof dish; top veal with mozzarella. Spoon tomato sauce over mozzarella.

3 Sprinkle evenly with parmesan; drizzle with remaining oil. Bake uncovered in moderate oven about 20 minutes or until golden brown.

TOMATO SAUCE Heat oil in medium frying pan; cook onion, celery, pepper and garlic, stirring until onion is soft. Push tomatoes with their liquid through sieve. Add pureed tomato to pan with sugar, paste and stock. Cover; bring to a boil. Reduce heat; simmer, covered, 30 minutes. Remove lid; simmer until sauce is thick. Stir through parsley and basil.

SERVES 4
PER SERVING 52.8G FAT; 3316KJ (792 CAL)

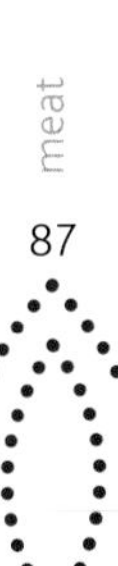

veal scallopini

PREPARATION TIME 10 MINUTES COOKING TIME 20 MINUTES

4 veal steaks (320g)
30g butter
1 small brown onion (80g), chopped finely
1/4 cup (60ml) dry sherry
2 teaspoons plain flour
1/2 cup (125ml) beef stock
125g button mushrooms, sliced thinly
2 tablespoons cream

1 Remove fat from veal; pound veal out thinly.

2 Melt butter in large frying pan; cook veal, while butter is foaming, about 3 minutes, turning once. Remove from pan; cook onion until soft. Pour in sherry.

3 Bring sherry to a boil. Stir in blended flour and stock; stir until sauce comes to a boil.

4 Return veal to pan. Add mushrooms; mix well. Cover pan; simmer gently 10 minutes. Stir in cream; stir until heated through.

SERVES 4

PER SERVING 13.8G FAT; 1206KJ (288 CAL)

pork steaks with baked pepper salad

PREPARATION TIME 20 MINUTES
COOKING TIME 1 HOUR 10 MINUTES

4 pork butterfly steaks (600g)
1/2 teaspoon cracked black pepper
1/2 teaspoon dried oregano
2 teaspoons olive oil
1 teaspoon cornflour
1 cup (250ml) chicken stock
2 teaspoons red wine vinegar

BAKED PEPPER SALAD
2 medium yellow peppers (400g)
2 large plum tomatoes (180g), halved
90g button mushrooms, sliced thinly
4 cloves garlic, crushed
1/4 teaspoon dried oregano
2 teaspoons olive oil
16 pitted black olives (80g)
2 tablespoons grated parmesan cheese

1 Sprinkle pork with black pepper and oregano. Heat oil in large frying pan; cook pork, until tender, turning once. Remove from pan.
2 Add blended cornflour and stock to pan; stir until mixture boils and thickens. Add vinegar; return pork to pan. Turn to coat in sauce.
3 Serve with baked pepper salad. Sprinkle with fresh oregano, if desired.

BAKED PEPPER SALAD Quarter peppers; remove seeds and membranes. Place peppers on oiled oven tray with tomato, mushrooms and garlic; sprinkle with oregano and oil. Bake, uncovered, in moderately hot oven 40 minutes. Add olives; sprinkle cheese over tomato. Bake further 15 minutes or until pepper is tender.

SERVES 4
PER SERVING 11.7G FAT; 1239KJ (296 CAL)
STORE RECIPE CAN BE MADE A DAY AHEAD AND REFRIGERATED, COVERED.

braised pork with fresh sage sauce

PREPARATION TIME 15 MINUTES COOKING TIME 1 HOUR 30 MINUTES

90g butter
1.5kg rack of pork (6 cutlets)
2 medium carrots (240g), sliced thickly
6 baby onions (150g), peeled
4 cloves garlic, peeled
2 bay leaves
6 sprigs fresh thyme
1 1/3 cups (330ml) dry white wine

FRESH SAGE SAUCE
15g butter
1 tablespoon plain flour
1 tablespoon fresh sage

1 Melt butter in large flameproof dish; cook pork until browned each side. Remove pork from dish. Place carrot, onion, garlic, bay leaves and thyme in dish; stir over heat about 5 minutes or until just browned. Return pork to dish with wine; transfer to moderate oven about 1 1/4 hours or until tender. Remove pork; keep warm.
2 Strain cooking liquid; reserve liquid. Discard vegetables.
3 Serve pork with sage sauce, roasted tomatoes and potatoes, if desired.

FRESH SAGE SAUCE Bring reserved liquid to a boil in medium saucepan; whisk in blended butter and flour. Boil, whisking constantly, until thickened slightly; stir in sage.

SERVES 6
PER SERVING 35.6G FAT; 2052KJ (490 CAL)

TIPS Ask your butcher to remove rind and tie pork well. Roast salted rind on rack in hot oven until crisp; serve with the pork.

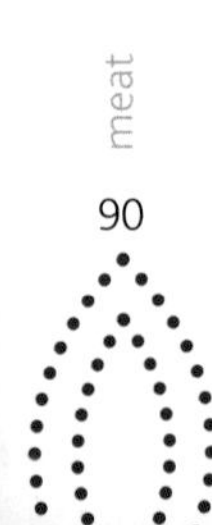

meatballs with chilli mushroom sauce

PREPARATION TIME 15 MINUTES
COOKING TIME 20 MINUTES

- 500g pork and veal mince
- 1 cup (70g) stale breadcrumbs
- 1/4 cup finely chopped fresh oregano
- 3 cloves garlic, crushed
- 1/3 cup (95g) tomato paste
- 1 egg, beaten lightly
- 1 tablespoon olive oil
- 250g button mushrooms, sliced thinly
- 850g canned tomatoes
- 1/4 cup (60ml) mild chilli sauce

1 Combine mince, breadcrumbs, oregano, garlic, paste and egg in medium bowl; roll level tablespoons of mixture into balls. Place meatballs on oiled oven tray; bake, uncovered, in moderately hot oven about 15 minutes or until cooked through.

2 Meanwhile, heat oil in large saucepan; cook mushrooms, stirring, until just soft. Add undrained crushed tomatoes and sauce to pan; bring to a boil. Reduce heat; simmer, uncovered, 5 minutes. Add meatballs; cook, stirring, 2 minutes.

SERVES 4
PER SERVING 16.4G FAT; 1649KJ (394 CAL)
STORE RECIPE CAN BE MADE 2 DAYS AHEAD AND REFRIGERATED, COVERED, OR FROZEN FOR UP TO 3 MONTHS.

calves liver with lemon and capers

PREPARATION TIME 10 MINUTES COOKING TIME 10 MINUTES

500g calves liver
1 tablespoon olive oil
60g butter
1/4 cup (60ml) lemon juice
1/2 teaspoon sugar
1 tablespoon baby capers
1 tablespoon fresh flat-leaf parsley leaves

1 Slice liver thinly; remove any membrane.

2 Heat oil and half of the butter in large frying pan. Cook liver quickly, over high heat, until browned all over and cooked as desired; remove from pan.

3 Add juice, sugar and remaining butter to pan; stir over medium heat until butter melts. Return liver to pan with capers and parsley. Cook, turning liver, until well coated and heated through.

SERVES 4

PER SERVING 27.6G FAT; 1538KJ (367 CAL)

TIP Ask your butcher to slice the liver thinly for you.

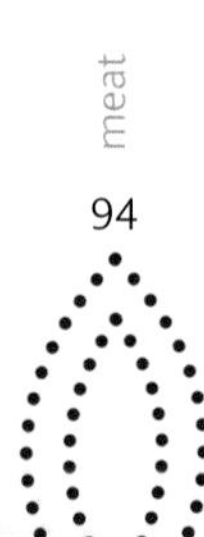

rib eye steak with roasted vegetables

PREPARATION TIME 10 MINUTES COOKING TIME 1 HOUR 20 MINUTES

2 medium red peppers (400g)
2 small aubergines (460g)
2 medium courgettes (240g)
6 beef rib eye steaks (1.3kg)
2 tablespoons olive oil
1/3 cup (60ml) olive paste

1 Quarter peppers; remove and discard seeds and membranes. Roast peppers under grill or in very hot oven, skin side up, until skin blisters and blackens. Cover pepper pieces in plastic or paper 5 minutes. Peel away skin; slice thickly. Cut aubergines into 2cm slices. Cut courgettes, lengthwise, into 2cm slices.
2 Cook steaks, in batches, on heated oiled griddle (or grill or barbecue) until browned both sides and cooked as desired. Cover to keep warm. Heat oil on grill plate; cook pepper, aubergine and courgette, in batches, until browned all over and soft.
3 Top steaks with pepper, aubergine and cougette and olive paste; drizzle with a little extra olive oil, if desired.

SERVES 6
PER SERVING 21.8G FAT; 1703KJ (407 CAL)

TIP Recipe best made just before serving.

chicken, lemon and artichoke skewers

PREPARATION TIME 20 MINUTES COOKING TIME 10 MINUTES

3 medium lemons (420g)
2 cloves garlic, crushed
1/4 cup (60ml) olive oil
600g chicken breast fillets, chopped coarsely
800g canned artichoke hearts, drained, halved
24 button mushrooms

1 Squeeze juice from one lemon (you will need two tablespoons of juice). Combine juice, garlic and oil in small screw-top jar; shake well.
2 Cut remaining lemons into 24 wedges. Thread chicken, artichoke, mushrooms and lemon onto 12 skewers. [Can be made a day ahead to this stage and refrigerated, covered.]
3 Cook skewers on heated oiled grill plate (or grill or barbecue) until browned all over and cooked through. Brush with oil mixture during cooking.

SERVES 4
PER SERVING 22.6G FAT; 1534KJ (366 CAL)

TIP If using wooden skewers, soak well in cold water before preparing.

chicken cacciatore

PREPARATION TIME 30 MINUTES COOKING TIME 1 HOUR 20 MINUTES

- 2 tablespoons olive oil
- 1.5kg chicken pieces
- 1 medium brown onion (150g), chopped finely
- 1 clove garlic, crushed
- 1/2 cup (125ml) dry white wine
- 1 1/2 tablespoons vinegar
- 1/2 cup (125ml) chicken stock
- 410g canned tomatoes
- 1 tablespoon tomato paste
- 1 teaspoon finely chopped fresh basil
- 1 teaspoon sugar
- 3 anchovy fillets, chopped finely
- 1/4 cup (60ml) milk
- 60g pitted black olives, halved
- 1 tablespoon finely chopped fresh parsley

1 Heat oil in large frying pan; cook chicken until browned all over. Place chicken in ovenproof dish.

2 Pour off most pan juices, leaving about 1 tablespoon in pan. Add onion and garlic to pan; cook until onion is soft. Add wine and vinegar; bring to a boil. Boil until reduced by half. Add stock; stir over high heat 2 minutes. Push tomatoes with their liquid through sieve; add to pan with paste, basil and sugar. Cook further 1 minute.

3 Pour tomato mixture over chicken pieces. Cover; cook in moderate oven 1 hour.

4 Soak anchovy in milk 5 minutes; drain on absorbent paper. Arrange chicken pieces on serving dish; keep warm. Pour pan juices into medium saucepan. Bring to a boil; boil 1 minute. Add anchovy, olives and parsley to pan; cook 1 minute. Pour sauce over chicken pieces. Sprinkle with extra chopped parsley, if desired.

SERVES 4

PER SERVING 42.2G FAT; 2572KJ (614 CAL)

chicken pancetta casserole

PREPARATION TIME 25 MINUTES
COOKING TIME 1 HOUR 20 MINUTES

2kg chicken thigh cutlets
2 tablespoons olive oil
12 slices pancetta (180g)
2 medium brown onions (300g), sliced thinly
2 cloves garlic, crushed
850g canned tomatoes
1/3 cup (95g) tomato paste
1 cup (250ml) dry white wine
2 cups (500ml) chicken stock
2 medium carrots (240g), chopped coarsely
1/3 cup finely chopped fresh flat-leaf parsley

1 Remove and discard skin from chicken.
2 Heat half of the oil in large saucepan; cook chicken, in batches, until browned all over.
3 Cut pancetta slices in half. Heat remaining oil in pan; cook onion, garlic and pancetta, stirring, until pancetta is browned.
4 Return chicken to pan with undrained crushed tomatoes, paste, wine and stock; bring to a boil. Reduce heat; simmer, uncovered, 30 minutes. Add carrot; simmer about 30 minutes or until carrot is tender. [Can be made a day ahead to this stage and refrigerated, covered, or frozen for up to 2 months.]
5 Stir through parsley just before serving. Serve with tiny new potatoes, if desired.

SERVES 8
PER SERVING 20.8G FAT; 1682KJ (402 CAL)

chicken parmesan with basil dressing

PREPARATION TIME 25 MINUTES COOKING TIME 20 MINUTES

2 cups (140g) stale breadcrumbs
1/3 cup (25g) finely grated parmesan cheese
2 tablespoons finely chopped fresh flat-leaf parsley
12 chicken tenderloins (750g)
3/4 cup (110g) plain flour
2 eggs, beaten lightly
250g curly endive
150g rocket

BASIL DRESSING
1 cup firmly packed fresh basil
1/2 cup (125ml) olive oil
1/4 cup (60ml) lemon juice
1 clove garlic, crushed

1 Combine breadcrumbs, cheese and parsley in medium bowl.
2 Toss chicken in flour to coat; shake away excess. Dip in egg, then in breadcrumb mixture to coat. Place on oiled oven trays. [Can be made a day ahead to this stage and refrigerated, covered, or frozen for up to 2 months.]
3 Bake in moderately hot oven, uncovered, about 20 minutes or until browned lightly and cooked through.
4 Serve chicken with endive and rocket; drizzle with basil dressing.

BASIL DRESSING Blend or process ingredients until combined. [Can be made a day ahead and refrigerated, covered.]

SERVES 4
PER SERVING 43.8G FAT; 3162KJ (755 CAL)

TIPS Make breadcrumbs from any stale bread (sourdough or ciabatta are both good). When blending or processing bread to make breadcrumbs, add parmesan and parsley at the very end of processing time, pulsing just a few times to combine the three ingredients thoroughly.

chicken osso buco

PREPARATION TIME 25 MINUTES COOKING TIME 1 HOUR 45 MINUTES

8 chicken thigh cutlets (1.3kg)
1/4 cup (35g) plain flour
2 tablespoons olive oil
1 large leek (500g), sliced thickly
2 cloves garlic, crushed
2 tablespoons tomato paste
2 1/2 cups (625ml) chicken stock
1/2 cup (125ml) dry white wine
400g canned tomatoes
3 trimmed sticks celery (225g), chopped coarsely
2 medium carrots (240g), chopped coarsely

GREMOLATA
1 medium lemon (140g)
1/4 cup finely chopped fresh parsley
2 cloves garlic, chopped finely

1 Remove and discard skin from chicken. Reserve 1 tablespoon of the flour. Toss chicken in remaining flour; shake off excess. Heat half of the oil in large saucepan; cook chicken, in batches, until browned all over.
2 Heat remaining oil in pan; cook leek and garlic, stirring, until leek is soft. Add reserved flour and paste; cook, stirring, 1 minute. Stir in stock, wine and undrained crushed tomatoes; bring to a boil.
3 Return chicken to pan. Reduce heat; simmer, covered, 1 1/4 hours. Add celery and carrot; simmer, uncovered, 20 minutes or until vegetables are soft. [Can be made a day ahead to this stage and refrigerated, covered.]
4 Just before serving, sprinkle with gremolata.

GREMOLATA Using vegetable peeler, remove rind from lemon. Cut rind into thin strips; chop finely. Combine lemon, parsley and garlic in small bowl; mix well.

SERVES 4
PER SERVING 15.6G FAT; 1971KJ (471 CAL)

grandmother's chicken

PREPARATION TIME 15 MINUTES COOKING TIME 1 HOUR 30 MINUTES

2 tablespoons vegetable oil
1 large brown onion (200g), sliced thickly
2 cloves garlic, crushed
4 chicken thigh cutlets (640g)
4 chicken drumsticks (600g)
4 sprigs fresh rosemary
4 medium potatoes (800g), chopped coarsely
2 medium tomatoes (380g), chopped coarsely
1/2 cup (125ml) chicken stock
150g button mushrooms, halved
4 bacon rashers, chopped coarsely
1/2 cup (80g) kalamata black olives

1 Heat oil in large flameproof baking dish; cook onion and garlic, stirring, until onion is soft. Add chicken; cook, stirring, until just browned all over. Add rosemary, potato, tomato and stock.
2 Bake, uncovered, in hot oven 1 hour. Stir in mushrooms, bacon and olives. Bake, uncovered, about 20 minutes or until chicken is tender.

SERVES 4
PER SERVING 45.5G FAT; 3117KJ (744 CAL)
STORE RECIPE CAN BE MADE 2 DAYS AHEAD AND REFRIGERATED, COVERED, OR FROZEN FOR UP TO 2 MONTHS.

chocolate cannoli

PREPARATION TIME 1 HOUR (PLUS REFRIGERATION TIME)
COOKING TIME 25 MINUTES

1 1/2 cups (225g) plain flour
2 tablespoons cocoa powder
2 egg yolks
1 egg, beaten lightly
2 tablespoons coffee-flavoured liqueur
1 tablespoon olive oil
1 1/2 tablespoons water, approximately
plain flour, extra
1 egg white
vegetable oil for deep-frying
16 strawberries

RICOTTA FILLING
1kg (5 cups) ricotta cheese
1/2 cup (80g) icing sugar
200g white chocolate buttons, melted
1/3 cup (80ml) coffee-flavoured liqueur

CHOCOLATE SAUCE
2/3 cup (160ml) cream
100g dark chocolate, chopped coarsely

1 Process flour, cocoa, yolks, egg, liqueur and olive oil with enough of the water to form a soft dough; process until mixture forms a ball. Knead dough on floured surface about 5 minutes or until smooth. Wrap in cling film; refrigerate 1 hour.
2 Divide dough into two portions. Roll each portion through pasta machine set on thickest setting. Fold dough in half; roll through machine, dusting with a little extra flour when necessary. Keep rolling dough through machine, adjusting setting so dough becomes thinner with each roll. Roll to second thinnest setting. Cut dough into 24 x 9cm-squares. Ensure each piece is 5mm short of the ends of the metal moulds or pieces of pasta.
3 Place whichever mould (see tip) you're using on end of each square.
4 Roll dough around mould; brush overlapping end with a little egg white. Make sure egg white does not touch the mould; press firmly to seal. Repeat with remaining squares.
5 Heat vegetable oil in large saucepan. Deep-fry cannoli, in batches, until crisp; drain on absorbent paper. Carefully remove warm cannoli shells from moulds; cool. [Can be made a day ahead to this stage and stored in airtight container.]
6 Spoon ricotta filling into large piping bag fitted with plain 1cm tube; pipe ricotta filling into cannoli. Serve chocolate cannoli with chocolate sauce and strawberries.

RICOTTA FILLING Beat cheese and icing sugar in large bowl with electric mixer until smooth; beat in cooled chocolate and liqueur. [Can be made a day ahead and refrigerated, covered.]

CHOCOLATE SAUCE Combine cream and chocolate in small saucepan, stir over low heat until chocolate melts.

SERVES 8
PER SERVING 43.1G FAT; 3129KJ (747 CAL)

TIP Cannelloni pasta shells make excellent cannoli moulds; they must be discarded after deep-frying. Metal cannoli moulds are available at specialty kitchen shops. If you use metal moulds, you're ensured of getting a sufficient number of moulds to make this recipe. You can substitute plain ready-made cannoli shells in this recipe.

cassata

PREPARATION TIME 1 HOUR (PLUS FREEZING TIME)

2 eggs, separated
1/2 cup (110g) icing sugar
1/2 cup (125ml) cream
few drops almond essence

CHOCOLATE LAYER
2 eggs, separated
1/2 cup (110g) icing sugar
1/2 cup (125ml) cream, beaten lightly
60g dark chocolate, melted
2 tablespoons cocoa powder
1 1/2 tablespoons water

FRUIT LAYER
1 cup (250ml) cream
1 teaspoon vanilla essence
1 egg white, beaten lightly
1/3 cup (55g) icing sugar
2 tablespoons finely chopped red glacé cherries
2 glacé apricots (40g), chopped finely
2 glacé pineapple rings (55g), chopped finely
1 tablespoon finely chopped green glacé cherries
1/3 cup (25g) flaked almonds, toasted

1 Beat egg whites in small bowl with electric mixer until firm peaks form; gradually beat in sifted icing sugar. Fold in lightly beaten egg yolks. Beat cream and essence in small bowl with electric mixer until soft peaks form; fold into egg mixture. Pour into deep 20cm-round springform cake tin. Smooth over top; freeze, covered, until firm.
2 Spread chocolate layer over almond layer; freeze, covered, until firm.
3 Spread fruit layer over chocolate layer; freeze, covered, until firm.
4 Run small spatula around edge of cassata; wipe a hot cloth over base and side of tin. Turn cassata onto serving plate; cut into wedges to serve. Sprinkle with extra glacé cherries, if desired.

CHOCOLATE LAYER Beat egg whites in small bowl with electric mixer until firm peaks form; gradually beat in sifted icing sugar. Beat cream in small bowl until soft peaks form; fold in egg white mixture. Place chocolate in small bowl; stir in egg yolks. Combine cocoa and the water in small jug; stir into chocolate mixture. Fold chocolate mixture through cream mixture.

FRUIT LAYER Beat cream and essence in small bowl with electric mixer until firm peaks form. Beat egg whites in small bowl with electric mixer until firm peaks form; gradually beat in sifted icing sugar. Fold egg white mixture into cream; gently stir through fruit and nuts.

SERVES 8
PER SERVING 34.6G FAT; 2016KJ (481 CAL)
STORE CASSATA IS BEST MADE A DAY AHEAD AND CAN BE FROZEN, COVERED, 3 DAYS.

zabaglione

PREPARATION TIME 10 MINUTES COOKING TIME 10 MINUTES

5 egg yolks
1/4 cup (55g) caster sugar
1/2 cup (125ml) sweet marsala
1/4 cup (60ml) dry white wine

1 Beat yolks and sugar in medium heatproof bowl with electric mixer until well combined.
2 Place bowl of mixture over medium saucepan of simmering water. Gradually beat in half of the marsala and half of the white wine; beat well. Gradually beat in remaining marsala and wine.
3 Beat constantly, about 10 minutes, or until thick and creamy. If mixture adheres to side of bowl, quickly remove from heat and beat vigorously with wooden spoon – especially around base. Pour into individual dishes; serve immediately.

TIP Zabaglione makes an excellent topping for fresh fruit.

SERVES 4
PER SERVING 7.7G FAT; 1160KJ (277 CAL)

lemon gelato

PREPARATION TIME 15 MINUTES (PLUS FREEZING TIME)
COOKING TIME 15 MINUTES (PLUS COOLING TIME)

1/2 cup (110g) caster sugar
1/2 cup (125ml) water
1/2 cup (125ml) sweet or dry white wine
1/2 cup (125ml) lemon juice, strained
1 egg white

1 Combine sugar, the water and wine in small saucepan; stir over low heat until sugar dissolves. Bring to a boil; reduce heat. Simmer, uncovered, 10 minutes; cool. Stir in juice; mix well. Pour into baking tin; freeze, covered, until mixture is just firm.

2 Remove from freezer. Turn mixture into medium bowl; beat until smooth with fork. Beat egg white in small bowl with electric mixer until firm; fold into lemon mixture. Return to tin; freeze until firm.

SERVES 2
PER SERVING 0.13G FAT; 1155KJ (276 CAL)
STORE GELATO IS BEST MADE A DAY AHEAD AND CAN BE FROZEN, COVERED FOR UP TO 3 DAYS.

tiramisu

PREPARATION TIME 25 MINUTES

2 tablespoons instant coffee
1¼ cups (310ml) boiling water
1 cup (250ml) sweet marsala
250g packet sponge-finger biscuits
½ cup (125ml) whipping cream
⅓ cup (55g) icing sugar
2 cups (500g) mascarpone cheese
40g dark chocolate, grated
125g blueberries

1 Dissolve coffee in the water in medium bowl. Stir in ⅔ cup (160ml) of the marsala; cool. Dip half of the biscuits, one at a time, in coffee mixture; arrange in single layer, in 2.5-litre (10-cup) glass dish.
2 Beat cream and icing sugar in small bowl until soft peaks form; fold in the mascarpone and remaining marsala.
3 Spread half of the cream mixture over biscuits in dish. Dip remaining biscuits in remaining coffee mixture; arrange on top of cream layer. Top biscuit layer with remaining cream mixture; sprinkle with chocolate. Cover; refrigerate several hours. [Can be made 2 days ahead to this stage and refrigerated, covered.]
4 Decorate top with blueberries, just before serving.

SERVES 6
PER SERVING 59.5G FAT; 3628KJ (867 CAL)

TIPS As with most desserts containing syrup, the flavour will develop more if made a day ahead and refrigerated, covered. Any type of berries are suitable for this recipe.

ricotta cake

PREPARATION TIME 1 HOUR COOKING TIME 1 HOUR (PLUS COOLING TIME)

370g packet chocolate cake mix
185g ricotta cheese
1/4 cup (55g) caster sugar
2 tablespoons Grand Marnier
30g glacé ginger, chopped finely
30g glacé cherries, chopped finely
30g dark chocolate, chopped finely
90g flaked almonds, toasted

SYRUP
2 tablespoons caster sugar
1/3 cup (80ml) water
2 tablespoons Grand Marnier

ICING
1/4 cup (55g) caster sugar
1/3 cup (80ml) water
125g butter
90g dark chocolate, melted

1 Make up cake mix according to directions on packet; spoon mixture into greased 23cm-round cake tin. Bake in moderate oven about 25 minutes or until cake is cooked when tested; turn onto wire rack to cool.
2 Push cheese through wire sieve into small bowl; beat with electric mixer until smooth and creamy. With motor operating, gradually beat in sugar and Grand Marnier, beating well between additions. Stir in ginger, cherries and chocolate; mix well.
3 Cut cake horizontally into three layers. Place one layer on serving plate; brush with syrup.
4 Spread half of the ricotta mixture over cake. Top with second layer of cake; brush with syrup. Spread with remaining ricotta mixture. Top with remaining layer of cake; brush with syrup.
5 Spread icing over top and side of cake; press nuts around side of cake. Refrigerate until ready to serve; stand at room temperature 10 minutes before serving. Cut into wedges to serve.

SYRUP Combine sugar, the water and Grand Marnier in small saucepan. Stir over low heat until sugar dissolves; allow to cool.

ICING Place sugar and the water in small saucepan. Stir over low heat until sugar dissolves; bring to a boil. Remove from heat; cool. Beat butter until soft and creamy; gradually beat in cooled syrup, a few drops at a time. Gradually add chocolate to butter mixture; beat until well combined.

SERVES 8
PER SERVING 31.3G FAT; 2418KJ (578 CAL)

TIP Ricotta cake is best made a day ahead and can be refrigerated, covered, 3 days.

zuppa inglese

PREPARATION TIME 1 HOUR (PLUS REFRIGERATING TIME)
COOKING TIME 50 MINUTES (PLUS COOLING TIME)

6 eggs, beaten lightly
1 1/4 cups (275g) caster sugar
1 cup (150g) plain flour
1/2 cup (75g) cornflour
1 1/2 teaspoons baking powder
2/3 cup (160ml) milk
2 tablespoons rum
500g strawberries
200g blueberries
200g raspberries
2 teaspoons icing sugar

CUSTARD FILLING
1/2 cup (75g) cornflour
1/2 cup (60g) custard powder
1/2 cup (110g) caster sugar
2 1/3 cups (580ml) milk
2 teaspoons vanilla essence
1 1/3 cup (300ml) whipping cream
30g butter
2 egg yolks

1 Beat eggs in medium bowl with electric mixer until thick and creamy. Gradually add sugar; beat until sugar dissolves. Gently fold in flour, cornflour and baking powder. Pour mixture into greased deep 28cm-round cake tin. Bake, uncovered, in moderate oven about 35 minutes or until cake is cooked when tested; turn onto wire rack to cool. Wash and dry cake tin.
2 Split cake, horizontally, into three even layers. Place first layer of cake in clean deep 28cm-round cake tin. Brush cake with combined milk and rum. Spread half of the custard filling evenly over cake. Reserve eight strawberries for decorating top of cake; hull and slice remaining strawberries. Sprinkle half of the sliced strawberries over custard layer. Place second layer of cake on top of strawberries; brush with rum mixture. Spread remaining custard filling evenly over cake; sprinkle with remaining strawberries. Top with third layer of cake; brush with remaining rum mixture. Refrigerate, covered, several hours. [Can be made 2 days ahead to this stage.]
3 Turn cake onto serving plate. Decorate top of cake with reserved strawberries, blueberries and raspberries; dust top with sifted icing sugar before serving.

CUSTARD FILLING Combine cornflour, custard powder and sugar in large saucepan. Gradually add milk; stir until smooth. Add essence and cream; stir until combined. Stir over low heat until custard boils and thickens; add butter. Simmer, uncovered, 3 minutes, stirring constantly; remove pan from heat. Add yolks; mix well. Transfer custard to medium heatproof bowl; cover surface with cling film. Allow to become cold; beat well.

SERVES 12
PER SERVING 41.1G FAT; 2815KJ (672 CAL)
STORE ZUPPA INGLESE IS BEST MADE A DAY AHEAD AND CAN BE REFRIGERATED, COVERED, 3 DAYS.

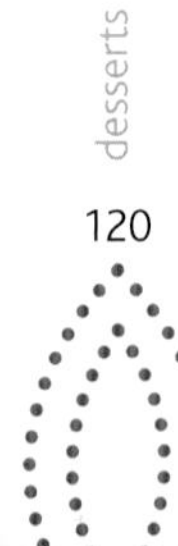

sicilian cheesecake

PREPARATION TIME 30 MINUTES (PLUS REFRIGERATING TIME)

185g plain chocolate biscuits, crushed finely
90g butter, melted
½ cup (125ml) cream
60g dark chocolate, grated coarsely

FILLING
625g ricotta cheese
1 cup (160g) icing sugar
1 teaspoon vanilla essence
2 tablespoons Crème de Cacao
2 tablespoons finely chopped mixed peel
60g dark chocolate, grated finely

1 Combine biscuit and butter in medium bowl; press evenly over base of 20cm-springform tin. Refrigerate while preparing filling.
2 Spoon filling over biscuit base; refrigerate at least 6 hours or overnight.
3 Just before serving, beat cream in small bowl with electric mixer until soft peaks form; spread evenly over top of cake. Sprinkle with chocolate.

FILLING Beat cheese, icing sugar, essence and Crème de Cacao in large bowl with electric mixer until smooth and fluffy. Add peel and chocolate; mix well.

SERVES 10
PER SERVING 27.4G FAT; 1816KJ (434 CAL)

poached peaches

PREPARATION TIME 5 MINUTES (PLUS REFRIGERATION TIME)
COOKING TIME 25 MINUTES

$1\frac{1}{2}$ cups (375ml) sauternes-style dessert wine
2 cups (500ml) water
1 cup (220g) caster sugar
1 strip lemon rind
6 medium peaches (1kg), washed

1 Combine wine, the water, sugar and rind in large saucepan; stir over low heat, without boiling, until sugar dissolves. Add unpeeled peaches; simmer, uncovered, about 20 minutes or until tender.
2 Remove from heat; cool. Transfer syrup and peaches to non-reactive bowl. Cover; refrigerate 3 hours.
3 Peel peaches; discard peel and lemon rind. Serve peaches with some of the syrup.

SERVES 6
PER SERVING 0.1G FAT; 1187KJ (284 CAL)

TIP If you choose peaches with a pink blush, poaching in their skins will intensify the blush on the peeled fruit.

mixed berries with mascarpone

PREPARATION TIME 10 MINUTES (PLUS REFRIGERATION TIME)

250g strawberries, quartered
200g raspberries
200g blueberries
2 tablespoons raspberry vinegar
$\frac{1}{4}$ teaspoon finely ground black pepper
$\frac{1}{2}$ cup (125ml) cream
200g mascarpone cheese
$\frac{1}{3}$ cup (55g) icing sugar

1 Combine berries, vinegar and pepper in large bowl. Cover; refrigerate 1 hour or until well chilled. [Can be made a day ahead to this stage.]
2 Whip cream in small bowl until soft peaks form; gently fold in mascarpone in two batches. [Can be made a day ahead to this stage and refrigerated, covered.]
3 Spoon mascarpone cream onto serving plates. Top with berry mixture, including any juices; dust thickly with sifted icing sugar.

SERVES 6
PER SERVING 28.4G FAT; 1380KJ (330 CAL)

honey grilled figs

PREPARATION TIME 5 MINUTES COOKING TIME 5 MINUTES

6 large figs (480g)
2 tablespoons caster sugar
1/4 cup (90g) honey
1 teaspoon vanilla essence

1 Gently break figs in half lengthways. Place figs on oven tray; sprinkle broken sides of figs with sugar.
2 Cook under hot grill about 5 minutes or until sugar melts and figs are browned lightly.
3 Meanwhile combine honey and essence in small saucepan; stir over low heat, without boiling, until honey is very runny.
4 Serve warm figs drizzled with honey mixture.

SERVES 6
PER SERVING 0.2G FAT; 425KJ (102 CAL)

TIPS Green or purple figs are suitable for this recipe. Serve with dollops of whipped mascarpone and cream.

frozen grapes

PREPARATION TIME 10 MINUTES (PLUS STANDING AND FREEZING)

500g green grapes
500g black grapes
1/4 cup (60ml) orange-flavoured liqueur

1 Wash grapes; remove stems. Cut grapes in half; remove pips. Combine in large bowl with liqueur. Cover; stand 1 hour.
2 Place grapes, cut-side down on freezer trays lined with baking parchment. Cover; freeze several hours or until firm. Transfer grapes to freezer container.
3 Serve from freezer.

SERVES 8
PER SERVING 0.2G FAT; 464KJ (111 CAL)
STORE RECIPE CAN BE MADE 3 MONTHS AHEAD

glossary

ALMOND
essence almond extract.
flaked paper-thin slices.
ANCHOVY FILLETS salted fillets; available rolled or flat and packaged or canned in oil.
ARTICHOKE HEARTS tender centre of the globe artichoke; sold in cans or loose, in brine.
AUBERGINE also known as egg-plant. Depending on age, they may require slicing and salting to reduce bitterness; rinse and dry well before using. Also baby aubergine.
BAKING POWDER a raising agent consisting mainly of 2 parts cream of tartar to 1 part bicarbonate of soda (baking soda).
BASIL an aromatic member of the mint family with both culinary and medicinal uses. There are many varieties, however, the most commonly used is sweet basil.
BAY LEAVES aromatic leaves from the bay tree; use fresh or dried.
BEANS
borlotti also known as roman beans; pale pink with dark red spots, eat fresh or dried.
dried cannellini small, dried white bean similar in appearance and flavour to great northern and navy or haricot beans.
dried haricot small, dried white bean similar in appearance and flavour to other *Phaseolus vulgaris*, great northern, navy and cannelloni beans.
BREADCRUMBS
packaged fine-textured, crunchy, purchased, white breadcrumbs; will keep almost indefinitely, in an airtight container.
stale also known as soft bread-crumbs; 1- or 2-day old bread made into crumbs by grating, blending or processing. Can be frozen for up to 6 months.
BUTTER use salted or unsalted ('sweet') butter; 125g is equal to 1 stick butter.
CALAMARI a type of mollusc; also known as squid. Slice hood thinly to form rings.
CALVES LIVER available from butchers; remove silvery membrane after rinsing.
CAPERS grey-green buds of a warm climate (usually Mediterranean) shrub, sold either dried and salted or pickled in a vinegar brine. The smaller capers are better.
CHICKEN
breast fillets breast halved, skinned and boned.
drumsticks leg with skin intact.
mince finely ground fresh chicken.
tenderloins thin strip of meat lying just under the breast; especially good for stir-fry cooking.
thigh cutlets thigh with skin and centre bone intact.
CHILLI
powder made from ground chillies; the Asian variety is the hottest. It can be used as a substitute for fresh chillies in the proportion of ½ teaspoon ground chilli powder to 1 medium chopped fresh chilli.
thai small, medium hot and bright-red to dark-green in colour.
CHIVES related to the onion and leek, with a subtle onion flavour.
CHOCOLATE, DARK eating chocolate; made from cocoa liquor, cocoa butter and sugar.
CLAMS we used a small ridge-shelled variety of this bivalve mollusc; also known as vongole.
COCOA POWDER ground cocoa beans with half of the butter removed.
COFFEE-FLAVOURED LIQUEUR Tia Maria, Kahlua.
CORIANDER also known as cilantro or chinese parsley; bright-green-leafed herb with a pungent flavour.
CORNFLOUR also known as cornstarch; used as a thickening agent in cooking.
COURGETTE also known as zucchini; green yellow or grey members of the squash family having edible flowers.
CREAM we used fresh cream in this book, unless otherwise stated. Also known as pure cream and pouring cream; has no additives unlike commercially thickened cream. Minimum fat content 35%.
sour a thick commercially-cultured soured cream good for dips, toppings and baked cheesecakes. Minimum fat content 35%.
whipping a cream containing a thickener. Minimum fat content 35%.
CURLY ENDIVE also known as frisee; a curly-leafed green vegetable, mainly used in salads.
CUSTARD POWDER powdered thickening agent used in custard; contains starch.
DARK RUM we prefer to use an underproof (not overproof) for a more subtle flavour.
DILL tiny green-yellow flowers with light green, feathery leaves.
DRIED YEAST a leavening agent used in breads.
FLOUR
plain white an all-purpose wheat flour.
self raising plain flour sifted with baking powder in the proportion of 1 cup flour to 2 teaspoons baking powder.
GARLIC a bulb contains many cloves which can be crushed, sliced, chopped, or used whole, peeled or unpeeled.
GINGER also known as green or root ginger; the thick gnarled root of a tropical plant.
GLACÉ FRUIT fruit preserved in sugar syrup.
GRAND MARNIER orange-flavoured liqueur based on Cognac-brandy.
HERBS we used dried (not ground) herbs in the ratio of 1 teaspoon dried herbs to 4 teaspoons chopped fresh herbs.
LEEK a member of the onion family; resembles the spring onion but is much larger.
MARSALA a sweet fortified wine originally from Sicily.
MILK we used full-cream homogenised milk unless otherwise specified.
MINT a tangy, aromatic herb available fresh or dried.
MIXED PEEL candied citrus peel.
MUSHROOMS
button small, cultivated white mushrooms having a delicate, subtle flavour.
flat large, soft, flat mushrooms with a rich earthy flavour; sometimes misnamed field mushrooms.

MUSSELS purchase from a reliable fish market. Mussels must be tightly closed when bought, indicating they are alive. Before cooking, scrub shells with a strong brush and remove 'beards'. Discard any shells that do not open after cooking.
MUSTARD, SEEDED French-style mustard with crushed seeds.
NUTMEG the dried nut of an evergreen tree native to Indonesia; available in ground form or you can grate your own with a fine grater.
OLIVE OIL mono-unsaturated; made from the pressing of tree-ripened olives. Extra light or light describes the mild flavour, not the fat levels. Extra virgin and virgin are the highest quality olive oils, obtained from the first pressings of the olive.
OLIVES
kalamata a dark olive, preserved in salt and oil; Greek in origin.
small stuffed green olives stuffed with pimento.
ONION
red also known as spanish, red spanish or bermuda onion; a sweet-flavoured, large, purple-red onion.
spring also known as scallion or (incorrectly) shallot; an immature onion picked before the bulb has formed, having a long, bright-green edible stalk.
ORANGE-FLAVOURED LIQUEUR Grand Marnier.
OREGANO a member of the mint family; related to but spicier than marjoram.
PARSLEY
curly most familiar variety with bright-green, tightly curled leaves.
flat-leaf also known as continental parsley or italian parsley.
PEPPER also known as bell pepper or capsicum; available in red, yellow and green varieties. Seeds and membranes should be discarded before use.
PEPPERCORNS available in black, white, red or green; we used the black dried variety.
PESTO made from garlic, oil, vinegar, pine nuts, basil, herbs and spices. Available bottled from supermarkets.
PINE NUTS also known as pignoli; small, cream-coloured kernels obtained from the cones of different varieties of pine trees.
PITTA also known as lebanese bread or pita; a wheat-flour pocket bread sold in large, flat pieces separating into two thin rounds.
PIZZA BASES commercially packaged, pre-cooked, wheat-flour round bases.
PORK
butterfly steaks skinless, boneless mid-loin chop, split in half and flattened.
rack row of cutlets.
POTATO, DESIREE long, oval potato; smooth pink skin with yellow flesh. Most suitable for salads, roasting, boiling and mashing; not suitable for frying.
PRAWNS also known as shrimp.
PUY LENTILS a very fine, dark blue-green, fast cooking lentil originally from Le Puy in France.
RICE, ARBORIO small, round-grain rice well-suited to absorb a large amount of liquid; especially suitable for risottos.
ROCKET also known as arugula, rugla and rucola; a peppery-tasting green leaf which can be eaten raw in salads or cooked in soups, risottos and the like.
SAFFRON stigma of a member of the crocus family; available in strands or ground form. Imparts a yellow-orange colour to food once infused. The most expensive spice in the world; keep refrigerated.
SALAMI
italian made from pork and red pepper; it is not spicy.
milano made from pork, garlic, white wine and peppercorns; quite spicy.
SARDINES small silvery fish with soft, oily flesh.
SAVOY CABBAGE large, heavy head with crinkled dark-green outer leaves; a fairly mild tasting cabbage.
SCALLOP a bivalve mollusc with fluted shell valve; we used scallops with the coral (roe) attached.
SEAFOOD MARINARA MIX a mixture of uncooked, chopped seafood available from fish markets and fishmongers.
SEMOLINA made from durum wheat; milled, various textured granules, all of these finer than flour. The main ingredient in good pastas and some kinds of gnocchi.
SPINACH Delicate, crinkled green leaves on thin stems; high in iron. Also, baby spinach.
SPONGE FINGER BISCUITS also known as savoiardi, savoy biscuits or ladyfingers; Italian-style, crisp biscuits made from a sponge-cake mixture.
SQUASH
butternut squash also known as butternut pumpkin.
patty-pan also known as scallopine or summer squash; small, flattish yellow or green-skinned squash.
STOCK 1 cup (250ml) stock is the equivalent of 1 cup (250ml) water plus 1 crumbled stock cube (or 1 teaspoon stock powder).
SUGAR
caster also known as superfine or finely granulated table sugar.
icing also known as confectioners' sugar or powdered sugar.
SUGAR SNAP PEAS small pods with tiny, formed peas inside; they are eaten whole, cooked or uncooked.
SWISS CHARD also known as silverbeet and mistakenly, spinach; a member of the beet family with tasty green leaves and celery-like stem.
THYME leaves have a warm, herby taste; can be used fresh or dried.
TOMATO
pasta sauce bottled prepared sauce available from supermarkets.
paste triple-concentrated tomato puree used to flavour soups, stews, sauces and casseroles.
puree canned pureed tomatoes (not tomato paste). Substitute fresh peeled and pureed tomatoes.
tomatoes
canned whole peeled tomatoes in natural juices.
plum also known as egg or roma, these are smallish, oval-shaped tomatoes much used in Italian cooking or salads.
sun-dried we used those bottled in oil, unless otherwise specified.
VANILLA ESSENCE we used imitation vanilla essence.
VEAL
shin also known as osso buco.
steaks schnitzel.
VEGETABLE OIL any number of oils sourced from plants rather than animal fats.
VINEGAR
balsamic a matured Italian vinegar; use sparingly.
raspberry made from fresh raspberries steeped in a white wine vinegar.
red wine based on fermented red wine.
white made from spirit of cane sugar.
white wine made from white wine.
WHITE FISH FILLETS any non-oily fish; bream, flathead, whiting, snapper, jewfish and ling. Redfish also comes into this category.

conversion charts

MEASURES

The cup and spoon measurements used in this book are metric: one measuring cup holds approximately 250ml; one metric tablespoon holds 20ml; one metric teaspoon holds 5ml.

All cup and spoon measurements are level. The most accurate way of measuring dry ingredients is to weigh them. When measuring liquids, use a clear glass or plastic jug with metric markings.

We use large eggs with an average weight of 60g.

WARNING This book contains recipes for dishes made with raw or lightly cooked eggs. These should be avoided by vulnerable people such as pregnant and nursing mothers, invalids, the elderly, babies and young children.

DRY MEASURES

metric	imperial
15g	1/2oz
30g	1oz
60g	2oz
90g	3oz
125g	4oz (1/4lb)
155g	5oz
185g	6oz
220g	7oz
250g	8oz (1/2lb)
280g	9oz
315g	10oz
345g	11oz
375g	12oz (3/4lb)
410g	13oz
440g	14oz
470g	15oz
500g	16oz (1lb)
750g	24oz (1 1/2lb)
1kg	32oz (2lb)

LIQUID MEASURES

metric	imperial
30ml	1 fl oz
60ml	2 fl oz
100ml	3 fl oz
125ml	4 fl oz
150ml	5 fl oz (1/4 pint/1 gill)
190ml	6 fl oz
250ml	8 fl oz
300ml	10 fl oz (1/2 pt)
500ml	16 fl oz
600ml	20 fl oz (1 pint)
1000ml (1 litre)	1 3/4 pints

LENGTH MEASURES

metric	imperial
3mm	1/8in
6mm	1/4in
1cm	1/2in
2cm	3/4in
2.5cm	1in
5cm	2in
6cm	2 1/2in
8cm	3in
10cm	4in
13cm	5in
15cm	6in
18cm	7in
20cm	8in
23cm	9in
25cm	10in
28cm	11in
30cm	12in (1ft)

OVEN TEMPERATURES

These oven temperatures are only a guide for conventional ovens. For fan-assisted ovens, check the manufacturer's manual.

	°C (Celcius)	°F (Fahrenheit)	gas mark
Very low	120	250	1/2
Low	150	275-300	1-2
Moderately low	170	325	3
Moderate	180	350-375	4-5
Moderately hot	200	400	6
Hot	220	425-450	7-8
Very hot	240	475	9

index

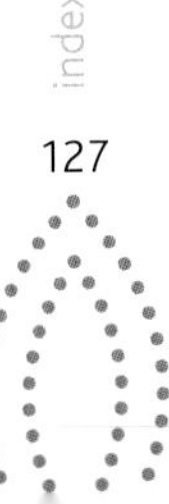